The Future of Politics
with the demise of the left/right confrontational system

Robert Corfe is not only a prolific writer on political and socio-economic topics, but is experienced in party political life both locally and on the national level. His successful journalistic career dates from the 1960s, and through extensive study, he has acquired considerable knowledge of the social sciences, history and philosophy. After a long business career in senior management in a manufacturing environment, promoting home-based productivity, and later as a management consultant, he founded the Campaign For Industry in 1987 to confront the damaging tendencies of international finance. Lord Gregson of Stockport was elected President of the association, and for over a decade Corfe wrote many pamphlets on the problems of industry and the question of more widely distributing the assets of wealth. His ten years in Scandinavia, in addition to business travels throughout the world, have given him a broad perspective of the needs of all humanity.

By the same author –

Social Capitalism in theory and practice

Vol. 1
Emergence of the New Majority

Vol. 2
The People's Capitalism

Vol. 3
Prosperity in a stable World

Egalitarianism of the Free Society
and the end of class conflict

The Death of Socialism
*the irrelevance of the traditional left & the call for a progressive
politics of universal humanity*

Populism Against Progress
and the collapse of aspirational values

Deism & Social Ethics
the role of religion in the third millennium

Freedom From America
*for safeguarding democracy & the economic & cultural integrity of
peoples*

Land of The Olympians
papers from the enlightened Far North

The Future of Politics

with the demise of the left/right confrontational system

Robert Corfe

Arena Books

First published in 2010 by Arena Books

Arena Books
6 Southgate Green
Bury St. Edmunds
IP33 2BL
01284 754123
www.arenabooks.co.uk

Corfe, Robert- 1935
The Future of Politics with the demise of the left/right confrontational system
1. Right and left (Political science) 2. Democracy -
I. Title
320'.011-dc22

ISBN-13 978-1-906791-46-9

BIC categories:- JPA, JPB, JPF, KCA, KND.

Printed and bound by Lightning Source UK

Cover design
by Jason Anscomb

Typeset in
Times New Roman

PREFACE

The implosion of the global financial system in 2007-2008 has been a slap in the face for the democratic rights of peoples worldwide, and this is an aspect of the ongoing crisis which hitherto has not been touched upon by leading commentators in the media. The enormity of the losses which exceed those of 1929, and promises to bring a catastrophe as great as that of the 1930s, has not yet struck the public consciousness.

The Institute for International Finance in Washington estimated that banks and insurance companies had written down more than $1,000 bn of credit losses, whilst the Bank of England suggested in Autumn 2008 that the total market losses on global credit assets had reached almost £3,000 bn which is a sum comparable to the annual output of the entire UK economy.

But the truly shocking aspect of the crisis is not simply the extent of the losses, for there have been almost comparable financial collapses before, but the senseless circumstances in which this has occurred. In the words of the financial author, Gillian Tett, "what makes the current drama so stunning, is that this disaster has not been triggered by any external event, such as war. Instead, over the past 18 months, the financial system seems to have collapsed in on itself – imploding, apparently, out of the blue. Groups that once seemed impregnable, such as Lehman Brothers, AIG, Northern Rock, Bear Stearns, Royal Bank of Scotland and Washington Mutual – to name but a few – have all disappeared, or virtually disappeared as independent entities. It's an outcome that almost no-one could have guessed at just a year before, and it's not over."[1]

The truth, then, is that the collapse was entirely self-inflicted through systemic failures within the financial system. It may be that the collapse was not (or possibly could not) be

---

[1] Gillian Tett, "Untangling The Crisis," *Management Today*, April 2009.

predicted by those working within the system, since firstly, they were so caught up within the self-enriching money-making process as to be blind to the possibility of a downside; and secondly, they were working for institutions of such a magnitude of strength, long established reputation, and invincibility, that the very notion of their vulnerability was unthinkable.

There were, however, many outside the financial system competent not merely to spot the dangers, but to predict with fair certainty that such an eventual collapse at some unknown date in the future was inevitable. The present author was one such person. If there were others in academia and elsewhere – and there were – who predicted eventual disaster, they were coolly dismissed by the political and financial establishments as Jeremiahs.

The financial institutions are therefore fully blameable for what has occurred. The crash cannot simply be dismissed as an "accident" – like a child dropping a pail of milk – because it wasn't. It occurred through a series of actions and events, both of which should have been clearly visible to their participants, which doomed the financial sector to certain catastrophe. Those within the industry were not so much the victims of hubris as guilty of preposterous stupidity brought on by blinding greed.

The governments of the leading world economies have not acted appropriately in the face of this crisis. They have chosen to bale out the banks and other institutions, and in this they have acted with discernment. They could not have acted otherwise as ordinary people would then have been unable to draw out cash, and the economies of the world would have ground to a halt. In this decision governments acted as they only could. But there their good responses came to a stop. The reality is that the leading governments of the world stepped back, appalled, unbelieving at what they saw, much like a parent confronted by the atrocious behaviour of a small child they knew not how to control.

And like a spoilt child that has been appeased, not many weeks later, after the taxpayer had contributed billions into an emergency fund to shore up the banks, and after the bankers had received a slap on the wrist for the "misbehaviour" of their overblown salaries, bonuses, and other perks, to the shocked astonishment of both the public and the government, the financiers, brokers, and all their tribe, were once again found to have their noses in the trough. On that occasion the government could do nothing except sit back sulkily and mumble about the greed of the undeserving.

But governmental inertia and nonchalance in the face of disaster on such a scale is unacceptable. Many questions are raised. Whilst on the one hand expressions of censure are wasted verbiage, on the other hand, government is afraid of initiating action of any kind. Intervention at once raises the bogey of moves towards "nationalisation," and so that must be stopped in its tracks; and then there is the fear of inexperience treading on unknown ground; but most of all, there is the insistence of the financial establishment that it alone is competent, or has a right, to attend to its own affairs. Of course there is the option of legislation to trim the edges of financial power, but all such moves have always been feeble or ineffective, and besides, encourage evasion.

A cursory review of the situation at once returns us to the opening sentence of this Preface. The financial establishment through its own internal business has brought ruin upon itself. In desperation it calls upon the government for help, and the taxpayer pays the penalty. If the financial establishment then insists on continuing to manage its own affairs as it wishes – or as it has done in the past – then that is clearly a slap in the face for the democratic rights of the general public. The fact is that the financial establishment has forfeited its right as an independent body through its own gross negligence and criminal greed. Why should the public be called upon to pay for its sins, or to sit back, passively awaiting the next financial collapse, when it will be called upon to pay up once again?

The public now has a moral right, through the generosity of its contribution, to participate in the management of the financial sector. Naturally, its first concern will be the transformation of financial systems in ensuring that no such crisis can re-occur, as otherwise, how can there be any assurance that no such event will be repeated? But such a call raises many issues. Clearly, nationalisation is not desirable. Financial systems must be made transparent and open to public inspection, and purged of many of their questionable methods and products. If the public are to take over the running of the financial establishment, and not merely the financial services they control, then this must not be as a socialistic-style representative collectivity, but directly as individuals with financial vested interests.

Any such proposals, of course, will raise immediate objections on the grounds that the financial sector is independent of government, and hence owned and managed as a private body only answerable to its members. And this raises the most important question of all. A situation has been reached in the evolution of society and our institutions when it has now become imperative to politicise the issue of our financial-industrial infrastructure. And the reason for this is that financial and corporate power has swallowed up the entire administrative and political systems in all the advanced industrial economies, and so has neutered what remains of democratic mechanisms.

This is a frightful prospect for the future of humankind, or for any kind of worthwhile freedom. But worse than this: governments are in denial about any such prospect. Furthermore, political parties of every hue, recede from any suggestion of intervening in the financial or corporate sectors – even after the catastrophic collapse of 2007-2008. When confronted, they either admit (with truth) they are incompetent for such a task, or else plead it is not their rightful sphere of activity to become involved in. The more significant explanation for this attitude, however, is that our politicians and civil servants are already in the pockets of these powerful financial interests.

Therefore, the question has to be asked: how can the peoples of the world be liberated from the tightening tentacles of plutocracy, and regain their democratic rights? The purpose of this book is to analyse the issues and present an answer. Politicising the world of corporate finance means opening it up for intelligent understanding and discussion as a political topic by all the political parties, planning for change, and then implementing necessary legislation. Such ideas, of course, are appalling to the ever-secretive world of high finance, and the latter can only respond with the blustering retort that, "finance is nothing whatsoever to do with politics, and that the topic is far too specialised and complex for politicians to start messing around in."

But finance *is* a political issue, and financiers have increasingly made it so through their own incompetence and outrageous expectation that the public should pay for their mistakes. If they can't manage their own affairs – which they clearly can't – then politics must intervene in the interests of us all. Any such proposals for change, of course, must be based on the authority of sound knowledge and experience, and this unfortunately, is sadly lacking in all political parties of the Anglo-Saxon economies. As from 4th November 2009, in Alistair Darling's latest bale-out of the banks, every family in Britain had a tax liability thrust upon them of £3,350 payable to the banks. On that date £25.5 bn was paid by the Treasury to the Royal Bank of Scotland, this being in addition to the 74 bn already paid to a group of leading banks including RBS, Lloyds, and HBOS. If these are not political issues, then what are?

A hundred years ago the nature of capitalism was the only major topic for Labour party discussion. Today it is the only topic which is forbidden. Capitalism in the 21st century is a taboo topic. The Labour party member attempting to raise the subject at a branch meeting becomes immediately suspect as a "Marxist" – irrespective of his personal views. Meanwhile, the parties of the right merely accept Rentier capitalism, with all its warts, as the only viable system which exists. Tories no more discuss the nature of capitalism than do their rivals, the socialists. It is just accepted, unthinkingly, and taken for granted.

This is something which has to change – and indeed, will change through the force of circumstances. But how this change will come about may take our politicians entirely by surprise. There is little use in approaching any of our existing parties for the kind of transformation needed. They just haven't the stomach for it. Change may come from an unexpected quarter – and it may be sudden.

Most political parties in the advanced industrial economies are already in a state of meltdown in terms of their membership collapse. Politicians realise this but they cannot comprehend the consequences – or choose not to do so. They imagine that the future will continue much as in the past, but of course it never does. History always springs an element of surprise on those too comfortable to endure the idea of change. The reality is that the left/right divide which has marked the process or dialectic for the evolution of democratic progress over the past 200 years is now coming to the end of its useful purpose. As this book shows, to attempt upholding the existing patterns of political life will be counter-productive in the future in advancing the best interests of the majority or humankind. There are many reasons for this, as discussed in the text which follows.

A new society is emerging. The old middle and working classes, and the values they represented, no longer exist – or are fast evaporating. This is something our politicians fail to understand, and have not accounted for. Although they try desperately to keep apace with events, their parties are still ideologically geared to addressing the old class system as it existed 60 or more years ago. They therefore have a vested interest in seeing society as it existed in a former era, as how else could they maintain the game of knockabout politics? Despite all conscious attempts to modernise, they remain inextricably trapped in a time-warp of the past. Hence, the confrontational attitudes of the left/right divide must go, as otherwise political issues in the future will be compounded rather than resolved for the longer term.

The new majority, denominated the middle-middle class, comprises 90%+ of the population in all advanced industrial economies. They are sick of the old politics and have clearly expressed their feelings in regard to this. Although highly heterogeneous, individualistic, and expressing a wide variation of views on all matters, they nonetheless share many common characteristics. This does not, of course, in itself identify them as a class. A superficial glance at the middle-middle majority might even indicate they have *none* of the characteristics properly defining a class. They do, however, share a number of distinctive economic interests, which mark them out as a group, and economic interests are the only criterion correctly defining a class.

These interests, interestingly, as we demonstrate clearly in this book, are not effectively promoted by any of the existing parties of either the left or right – and certainly not the centre. All this exposes the need for a fresh view of politics. Linked into the unrepresented economic needs of this new majority is the necessity of transforming our financial-industrial infrastructure. This, in part, explains the blind spot of political parties today. The new majority does not, as yet, have a political consciousness of its existence, but this will emerge as inevitably as dawn follows the blackness of night, irrespective of any intellectual exercise to help it on its way.

As it gains political consciousness, the middle-middle majority will mutate into the all-powerful knowledge-enriched Responsible Society. In this role, through the advantages of the open society – which even now is pressing in all directions for greater information rights – it will take over the means of production, distribution, and the means of exchange.

This would be achieved through the *direct* democratic means of individual participation which minimises the disadvantageous dilution of people power through the mesh of representative bodies. As with any social change, those of the Responsible Society would be endowed with characteristics and values quite different from their forebears, as also they would differ from those of socialism or present day Conservatism. Such changes are already noticeable through the huge transformation of society and the world of work over the past 60 years.

They would be values reflecting the totality of a people not confronted by the threat of class enmity, and hence, through the self-assurance which follows from this, there would be an independence of spirit, a high priority for education and natural intelligence, and a fearless will in advancing the cause of social justice and upwardly aspiring egalitarianism. Of course there would be political differences in society, but these would be settled predominantly between functional groups through a new mode of effective democracy as described in this book.

In this way we have come, via a circuitous route, to hazard an answer to those questions posed near the start of this Preface: viz., how best to challenge the overbearing power of the financial institutions and absorb them within the democratic will of the majority? And what measures are preferable in safeguarding against the repetition of the financial collapse of 2007-2008, and all the turmoil this brings to the lives of peoples worldwide?

In this book we have therefore attempted to outline the foundations for an individualistic people-powered society, regaining its democratic roots, on the demise of confrontational left/right politics, which is now unable to take us any further towards a positive or constructive future.

Robert Corfe
February 2010

CONTENTS

CONTENTS

CHAPTER 7
The unrepresented middle-middle majority is the political and democratic hope for the future

CHAPTER 8
The profitable Productive economy must displace Rentier capitalism

CHAPTER 9
The knowledge-based new majority as the foundation stone for a just and equitable world

CONTENTS

CHAPTER 10
The Rationale for the Full democracy of the future

CHAPTER 1
The futility of the left/right divide in resolving the problems of today and tomorrow

"The true philosopher does not attempt to narrow down the world to fit his understanding, but strives to expand his understanding of the world."

Richard Tarnas, *The Passion of The Western Mind,*
Ballantine Books, NY, 1991, p. 275.

1 – The silent death of democracy 2 – Averting the dangers of discontent 3 – Spin as the desperation of impotent government 4 – Left/right politics has lost its usefulness 5 – The unsuspected threat to the political establishment 6 – Disillusionment of those who live in the political past 7 – Disillusionment of the realist majority

1 – The silent death of democracy

This book is addressed to all those with an interest in political issues, to the broader electorate no less than to activists committed to local or national politics, and irrespective of where the individual may nominally or actually (in the recesses of his heart) place him or herself within the spectrum of the left/right divide.

This broad address is made to all sectors of our heterogeneous society because the confrontational system in its present form throughout the industrialised world, in both East and West, has outlived its useful purpose in meeting the crises of the future, or resolving successfully for the longer term the major questions of the present day. Hence these are matters which touch the interests of us all.

It may be an exaggeration to contend there has been a *breakdown* of the democratic system, although this term is often used in expressing hopelessness or pessimism in the light of widespread apathy, or in describing the want of connectedness between the people and their rulers. A breakdown suggests rather the onset of anarchy or revolution, which is not the case in the contemporary world. It would be more accurate to contend there has occurred a *silent death* of the democratic system. It has occurred not through the intended actions of any political sector in society, but rather through a complex set of socio-economic factors beyond the will or anticipation of any group exerting power in public life. The causes of this silent death have been analysed in some depth in my book, *Emergence of The New Majority*, and will not be repeated here.

No one doubts what is commonly, even if inaccurately, described as the "breakdown" of the political system. It is made most evident through the collapse of political party memberships, and worse still, the declining percentages of those prepared to cast a vote, or fulfil their democratic obligations in the community. Research has shown that the decline of democratic participation tends to stem from two opposing situations: either contentment or complacency with the status quo, or disillusion and anger with the powers that be, and today it is the latter which is significant.

From a purely British perspective, that acute observer of the political scene, Andrew Rawnsley, has noted that, "we are accustomed to viewing the political struggle as a seesaw. When the Tories are declining, Labour has to be advancing. When Labour slumps, the Tories must be buoyant. This bipolar view of politics will no longer do as an explanation for where we are …"[2] Further on in the same article, he explains this through tracing the historical divide between the electorate and their representatives, arguing that, "beneath those short-term effects is a much longer and deeper trend of voter alienation from the two big parties. This can be traced back over the past 60 years. In the election of October 1951, when Winston Churchill battled Clement Attlee for the premiership, more than 96% of British voters supported either the Conservatives or Labour. You were a member of a tiny club if you preferred the Liberals or one of the minor parties.

"That was the high water mark of the two-party domination of Britain. At the February and October elections of 1976, when Harold Wilson competed with Ted Heath, support for the big two had fallen to 75%. By May 2005, when Tony

---

[2] Andrew Rawnsley, "Labour may never, ever win power on its own again," *The Observer*, 19th July 2009.

Blair contended with Michael Howard, barely more than two-thirds of the voters supported their parties. There were many more people who didn't vote than there were willing to make a cross for either Labour or the Tories.

"This long-term decline has disturbing - even terrifying – implications for both parties. It challenges the electoral system which they have relied on to sustain their duopoly. First past the post was just about defensible as a method of selecting governments when elections were essentially a two-horse race. It looks more anarchic and illegitimate when a large and growing proportion of the electorate doesn't want to be represented by either Labour or the Tories."

Another leading commentator, Adrian Hamilton, has written recently that, "every political leader in Britain starts by saying they're going to move away from Punch and Judy politics. Gordon Brown did it when he became Prime Minister, going as far as trying to create a ministry of all the talents, regardless of party. David Cameron made a great virtue of his wish to be consensual wherever possible when he became leader of the opposition. And we all know what happened to that promise. At the first whiff of an election, we're back to the slanging matches with a real vengeance.

"Adversarial politics are supposed to draw out difference and illuminate options. That's what the game is said to be ultimately about. But the extraordinary thing about the British party debate at the moment is that on virtually all the key issues there is no worthwhile difference between the two main parties. Indeed, the increasing concentration of public argument into a ding-dong between Labour and Tory is actually serving to reduce understanding rather than increase it. This is not about the usual accusation that the two parties barely differ in their centrist thinking. They don't. On most specifics the two main parties are deeply divided in approach if not outcome."[3]

The last two sentences are profoundly significant in indicating there is something seriously malfunctional yet

---

[3] Adrian Hamilton, "Two-Party Politics is doing us no good," *The Independent*, 20th August 2009.

inexplicable in our party political system: the parties are strangely similar yet deeply at odds. The sentiments above, of Rawnsley and Hamilton, are typical of opinions held by informed commentators throughout the media, but unfortunately, their analyses do not begin to uncover the true situation. The reality, as revealed in this book, is that all the parties are now confronted by issues of a magnitude and nature they cannot and do not wish to tackle. Their response is to brush such issues under the carpet, and the crazy confusion and illogicality of their conflict is merely a psychological symptom of their state of denial. But this particular pathology of our time is not confined to Britain. It will be found throughout all the advanced industrial economies in both East and West.

This breakdown or "silent death" of the political system is also reflected by a surge in the hypocrisy, pretence, and corruption of political life to a degree beyond which the public is prepared to tolerate without deep disillusion and withdrawal from participation in the political process. In all ages, in most territories, there has always existed a sceptical attitude towards politicians and their motives. This is not only natural but inevitable due to the conflict of economic interests within any community, but when such cynicism exceeds a certain level, and is reflected through a growing divide between the ruled and their masters, and by the presence of what might objectively be described as *bad government* in serving majority needs, then a politically pathological situation may be deemed to exist.

2 – Averting the dangers of discontent

In a pre-democratic world when government was less sensitive to heeding public opinion, when the ruled may have felt too readily the hand of oppression, or when economic crises of one kind or another could not be averted, then riots or rebellions, or even revolution, was the frequent consequence. But today such dramatic episodes are uncommon – at least in the developed world. This is because the governments of the industrialised economies, under the guidance of democratic institutions, have developed to perfection a set of manipulative skills which have never been exceeded in previous epochs. Although the purpose of democracy is to fulfil the will of the people, or the majority of the electorate, it is doubtful if as yet it has fully succeeded in this in any realistic sense, primarily because the will of the people is not clearly definable. What democracy succeeds in accomplishing with masterful effect is assuaging discontent and creating the appearance of well-being and stability – and such palliatives are at the present time most energetically promoted through the fine art of spin-doctoring. And it is only to be expected that failing democracies should find themselves performing such a role.

The promotion of contentment as against promoting the better or wiser interests of humankind is not entirely the invention of the modern world, for "bread and circuses" were the gift of the wealthy to the masses in the ancient world in ensuring order and a more passive population. But the crude efforts of Roman administration cannot possibly be compared with the sophisticated subtleties and wide-ranging strategies of contemporary governments in manipulating societies in the 21st century. Modern governments do not seek to de-sensitise the masses through debasing their moral conscience with gladiatorial combats and all the cruelties of the Roman amphitheatre, so that the majority have little time or inclination to reflect on questions of justice or changing the status quo.

Modern governments may be less crude, but they are far more hypocritical and scheming in their manipulation of the populace – and they utilise the well-developed theories of psychology and the social sciences in achieving their questionable ends. Powerful financial-industrial elites, with the helping hand of legislation, go to great lengths in ensuring that ordinary people do not speculate on matters beyond the limiting parameters of establishment thinking. Perhaps of greatest significance are the huge subsidies and tax allowances awarded to spectacular sporting activities – to activities which have expanded out of all recognition over the past hundred years in tandem with the expansion of popular democracy.

The blight of spin-doctoring is not only that it is used for specific purposes, or diverts attention from troubles which government wishes to cover up, or that it corrupts the democratic process through confusion or falsehood, but that it penetrates every nook and cranny of political life. When modern manipulation becomes a habit, politicians end up by deceiving themselves, because such manipulation takes on a higher priority in the busy life of politics than the resolution of substantive issues themselves. The deceit of spin-doctoring enters into the heart of policy-making when compromise or costs call for cut-backs or undesirable changes, and these are covered up by the gloss of rhetoric.

A prime example of such deception may be observed from the outcome of New Labour's great cry from 1997 onwards of, "Education, education, education!" It became the commonly held belief that the Labour party had set about improving the educational system to fit the demands of our fast-changing society, but it was subsequently revealed that over the following years they damaged every level of the educational system and worsened the prospects for our employment-creating industrial future. The ideological motivations and practical outcome of Labour's educational policies have been examined in my book, *The Death of Socialism*, and also in its predecessor, *Populism Against Progress*.

3 – Spin as the desperation of impotent government

This brings us directly from the question of the manipulation of information, for the purposes of electoral success, to the pattern of spin-doctoring in ineffective or decaying democracies when linked to poor government. Spin-doctoring or the manipulation of the electorate always has a deceptive dimension, which at the simplest level may comprise the exaggeration of its promises in conjunction with enlarging on the alleged faults of the opposition, but it may then extend to covering up its own motives and intentions to propagating in a rush all kinds of ideas or policies which may never – or could never see the light of day.

Over the past few decades it is certain that objectively conceived worsening government has been linked to an increasing level of spin-doctoring or what was at one time straightforwardly described as propaganda. The evidence of bad government has most clearly been made evident by two factors: firstly, through ill-thought out or incompetent "sound bite" legislation which fails to achieve what was originally intended; and secondly, the related factor of legislation which compounds existing problems through compiling complexity on top of complexity. Examples of this are soon identified in looking at the red tape imposed on teachers, policemen, or health workers, when the latter should be concentrating on the purposes of their function.

How has all this come about? It cannot simply be written off as the "incompetence" of politicians or their civil servants on grounds of insufficient intelligence or poor training. Our politicians may be blamed for all kinds of faults directly linked to their legislative or executive functions but such faults are rarely and unlikely to be associated with lack of intrinsic foresight or poor judgement, or deviations of personality. Most such faults may instead be traceable ultimately to deviations in perceiving reality and true values, arising from a pattern of conflict which has now lost its utility in resolving issues effectively. This occurs through a particular kind of compromise which is negative rather than positive. In such a situation, all becomes deception and scuttling into expediency.

The truth of our political plight, therefore, needs to be sought not in examining individuals – who cannot and are hardly likely to reveal anything significantly noteworthy about their motives – but in examining socio-economic systems which mould and manipulate politicians to fit the demands of their own pattern of activity. Hence politicians are obliged to follow the set pattern of systems rather than their own personal will or choice of direction. It is an irony that the politically-interested public turn to political biographies in their attempt to grasp reality, where they glean little about the real motives of decision-making, when instead they should turn to studying the power of the knowledge-based society and the secret strategies of hidden forces which hold political systems in their grip. The political system may indeed stand nominally at the apex of society, but it is powerless and at the mercy of a greater master. Ask any MP the influence he purports to exert and he will readily admit to being little more than a eunuch.

Great or heroic epochs in the history of humankind are those when leading individuals and governments exert a positive will and drive policies which are comprehended and sanctioned by their peoples. Declining or crisis-ridden epochs, on the other hand, are ruled by those who have little real control over events, and consequently are forced into putting up a pretence of swaying real power. The spin-doctoring, hypocrisy, and manipulation of electorates engaged in by all the great parliamentary movements of our time worldwide, are not a symptom of Machiavellian ingenuity of powerful administrations in achieving great purposes, but rather symptoms of strategic withdrawal by those who are both uncertain of their strength and what they really want to achieve. It is hence a form of deceit reflecting weakness – a rearguard face-saving strategy of little credit to its desperate practitioners.

4 – Left/right politics has lost its usefulness

The crisis of contemporary politics stems from the transformation of society and the world of work over the past 60 years, and the failure of parliamentary parties across the political spectrum to keep abreast of these dramatic changes. Political ideologies or those essential theories, which alone form a connecting link between governments and the people whom they rule, or between representatives and their electorates, have failed to progress in tandem with the real or practical world. The great ideologies, or competing theories of good government or justice have become locked into a time-warp of the past. This is a situation already acknowledged by percipient opinion-formers, and it is fully understood by activists of all leading groups – although for obvious reasons they are reluctant to raise it publicly as a discussion topic. It is a problem which has only manifested its existence over the past few decades. It is, therefore, an unprecedented issue which calls for urgent resolution. How has it come about and what is the answer?

It is no mysterious phenomenon. It springs directly from the practical "breakdown" or failure of our democratic system to perform the traditional function to which it was accustomed. Existing politics throughout the modern industrialised world have for two hundred years been dependent on the practical interactions of the left/right divide, and now the justification for such a system is coming to an end. Its rationale is no longer capable of advancing progress. It can no longer deliver the social and other benefits for which it originally came into existence. And yet we still live in a world where the non-existence of the left/right divide continues to make politics unthinkable. This perhaps is the greatest conundrum confronting humankind in the 21st century.

The Hegelian dialectic of progress of thesis, antithesis, and synthesis, which Marx interpreted in the materialistic terms of the class struggle, has long since been accepted across the entire political spectrum as the basis of progress, and as a sound platform for democratic activity. And this is especially the case with confrontational or two-party representative systems, as in Britain or America, which look askance or even a sneer at the participatory systems on the Continent or elsewhere, as not being "properly workable" or "exerting definitive power," and too liable to indecision, weakness, and the kind of corruption which stems from excessive compromise.

The Mother of Parliaments is still looked-up to by the nations of the world as the ideal democratic system, with its cross-benches and knockabout style – so different from the "mealy-mouthed muddle and confusion" of the circular-formed chamber. The British or *original* parliamentary system (and anyway, the latter contention is far from true) is admired for its directness and abrasive candour kept in balance by equable manners and the toleration of difference, as contrasted with the often exclusive parochialism so frequently found in multi-party systems. But the confrontational system is now bankrupt as a mode in advancing the progress of society, or even in maintaining efficient government on a day-to-day basis, since its grounds for confrontation have become a lie, and have degenerated into a game of pretence and hypocrisy. And this has never been more clearly demonstrated than during the Wednesday Question time sessions of the British House of Commons.

5 – The unsuspected threat to the political establishment

But worse than this has occurred: for the very topics of parliamentary debate have become peripheral to causal problems underlying the real unrecognised issues of our age. These real issues, meanwhile, are questions of little interest to our politicians or elected representatives, since supposedly they have "little mileage," or are matters which are off their "radar screen," as they fail to fit within their age-old ideological party frameworks. The same dated framework and discredited intellectual mindset applies equally to those states governed by multi-party or participatory systems of democracy.

Over the past few years innumerable articles have appeared in our leading journals and broadsheets by prominent opinion-formers decrying the barrenness of contemporary political thought, and pondering in mystified wonder how such an intellectual wasteland could exist in a world facing ever-greater crises on many fronts. All these opinion-formers, it seems, are too obtuse to observe and draw conclusions from the consequences of the socio-economic transformation which has changed the advanced industrial world over the past 60 years. The cause for our present ills, if not the answer to their resolution, stares us in the face.

It might even be argued that the task of democratic struggle has already fulfilled the greater part of its purpose in resolving the great questions of social justice and egalitarianism. Furthermore, by those on the left, it might be demonstrated that the leading industrialised economies, in both East and West, are now approaching that crucial historical point when the "proletariat" will take over the means of production, distribution, and the means of exchange, and overthrow the hated forces of oppression. Such a millenarian epoch, however, may come to pass but in a guise far different from the Marxist vision, and the "proletariat" of today's reality may seem to contradict all the aspirations and appearances so dear to the predictions of traditional Marxism or the followers of socialist ideology. All this, of course, only helps to throw our progressive intellectuals into confusion when confronted by the world of actuality. The truth is that they cannot believe – or refuse to accept – the plain facts as they exist.

Few prognostications of the future are realised as originally imagined or described, and those that materialise most closely, as envisaged by their intelligent inventors, are manifested so differently from the original idea as almost to be unrecognisable. There has emerged in the 21st century a highly heterogeneous class – i.e. heterogeneous in terms of culture, race, religion, attitudes, and in every other aspect – except for one highly significant characteristic. And that single characteristic concerns the underlying economic interests of that class – and when all is said and done, economic interests are the only *true* defining interests of a class.

As this new class represents the 90%+ majority in any advanced industrial economy, it must therefore present a huge potential threat to the status quo. Its political power, if organised, must therefore be immense. Its possible threat to the financial-industrial establishment and the rigid conservatism of the political system cannot but be overwhelming. On the other hand, its heterogeneity may be seen as a divisive factor which defies any attempt at unity or movement towards a course of common cooperation. This new class may be denominated the middle-middle majority, comprising those who have emerged from the cloth-capped proletariat to enjoy a more affluent life-style, to those who have sunk from rare privilege and affluence, to a more modest but comfortable livelihood within two generations, and all those who exist between these two given points.

6 – Disillusionment of those who live in the political past

At first sight, such a mixture of all and sundry could hardly be described as comprising a *class* of any kind by any stretch of the imagination. Moreover, a glance at their political opinions might further indicate a state of longstanding division and conflict. Whilst many of the upwardly mobile may be assumed to have sufficient compassion for their antecedents to be sympathetic to the left, those who have fallen from a greater height, may be assumed to have a sufficient memory of the past to desire a reversal of their fate.

Both such political tendencies howsoever they may be commonly held, would reflect a reactionary view of the world, both sentimental and unreal. Fortunately, in the enlightened industrial world, the majority are forward-looking rather than backward-looking, not necessarily through conscious choice, but through the need in facing the facts of survival. Homo sapiens is necessarily adaptable in a social context, and will change through human necessity in harmonising with those around them in maximising their better chances in life.

Whilst those who have bettered their material circumstances, through a mix of personal effort and changing socio-economic conditions, whilst retaining a mindset harking back to an ancestral past may be described as "genetically" fixed within a class-based framework; so likewise may those dreamy sentimentalists who boast about the social status of their parents or grandparents. In the contemporary or real world both such attitudes from the opposite ends of society may be described as *pathological* in the sense of escapism and failure to meet with their own best needs in present circumstances. Both fail to maximise their opportunities as individuals – or are liable to do so – in the socio-economic world as they find it. Whilst those from a privileged past are often ridiculed by their friends, or sniggered at behind their backs, if not dismissed as "degenerate" because of their fall from grace; those from a proletarian background may simply be dismissed in failing to keep abreast with changes in a progressing world.

These two mindsets, or their variations, may still appear as recurring types amongst political activists within our outdated confrontational parliamentary system, but when they do emerge in their true colours, they are usually despised even by the majority of their colleagues, the latter who nonetheless attempt to maintain a level-headedness within this failing system. Such persons, as we have described, represent a small minority, but are visible beyond their number from the very fact of their eccentricity or outrageousness.

More common, but hardly less reprehensible, however, are those who have reacted against their past in a more pointed manner in an attempt to repudiate everything which their forebears represented. The most common type falling into such a category is *Essex* man or woman, i.e. those with usually strong right wing or Thatcherite views, who have given a bad name to the essential value of individualism through callousness or disdain for the disadvantaged and downtrodden. These are people often obsessed with money-making above other priorities, and are unconcerned with how money is made, or the abuses of usury.

They often regard their parents or grandparents with mildly bemused disdain, as those who are "out of touch" with the world, and whose values or opinions are of little consequence for the future. As advocates of meritocracy they were often keen supporters of the New Tory party in the 1980s and 90s, in pursuing an economics which refused to recognise the concept of "society." At the opposite end of the spectrum are those from a privileged background, who filled with disgust at the bourgeois values of their antecedents, labelled themselves as the new "proletariat" and joined the intelligentsia of the left in promoting class struggle as the only "practical" path towards a more just and egalitarian society. Both these latter types are no less deluded in their grasp of reality than the older type conservatives of both left and right described on previous pages.

8 – Disillusionment of the realist majority

The vast majority of people, say 90%, do not fall into any of the four categories outlined above. Instead, they are disillusioned with all parties, and whilst holding their own highly individualistic views, many will nonetheless cast a vote from time to time, either in an attempt to oust a particular party, or because any change in itself is regarded as a good, or because a particular phrase or politician of the moment happens to take their fancy. The majority in the industrialised world are moderate and liberal in their views, and sufficiently pragmatic in their day-to-day lives to meet the world on the terms which the latter dictates. Hence the majority are determinists and few would admit the ability of exerting sufficient free will in fulfilling their deepest aspirations. In the sphere of political or democratic activity this reflects a deep misgiving not only with government but with the financial-industrial infrastructure, the latter dictating its own terms to the former.

Throughout the industrialised world today electoral politics has become a negative rather than a positive activity. That is, we may be empowered to express our disdain for policies and politicians we despise, but we are denied the possibility for expressing our political desires or needs. This is a highly unsatisfactory situation which calls for a scientific explanation. We cannot simply blame our politicians, although the circumstances in which we presently find ourselves may only succeed in calling forth those with second rate minds, or those who are so deficiently percipient we can hardly trust their judgement. In other words, it is argued that those in positions of great power lacking in sufficient knowledge and expertise, or intellectual understanding, are also those who fail as human personalities through no real fault of their own. They are rather victims of their own tragedy or circumstances, and that is the fate of today's political elite. The breakdown of democratic government is due to the unseen movement of the tectonic plates shifting the socio-economic system in all directions and affecting every sector of society.

Every epoch of history, for some unknown reason, seems to summon the leaders it deserves, so that in times of stability, prosperity, and success, wise and benevolent leaders emerge to exert an almost omnipotent power; whilst in times of economic failure or rampant chaos and destruction, the stupid and corrupt are always there in positions of leadership. We may rest assured that amongst the sullen politically inactive 90%+ majority of the industrialised economies of the world, there already exists, lying hidden in every nation state, many with the imaginative potential or force of character of a Cavour, a Bismarck, an Atatürk, or a Lee Kuan Yew, to save their peoples in their hour of need.

But such individuals lie dormant and politically inactive for the sound reason that they remain contemptuous of contemporary political life; and instead of soiling their hands or demeaning their reputations through involvement with political parties with discredited and outdated ideologies, they would prefer to put their energies into the spheres of commerce or academia. Hence, they possess an innate intelligence and social awareness which puts the thought of a political career beyond the pale. All this reflects the age-old truth that success breeds success, whilst failure only generates failure, but it raises the assertion from the level of the individual to that of the social system.

CHAPTER 2
The widening divide between the people and their rulers

"Interviews with presidents, or other decision-makers are usually unrewarding, for the obvious reason that most of what such people say is for the public record."

Eric Hobsbawm, *Age of Extremes*, Michael Joseph, 1994, p. x.

1 – The demise of the left/right political conflict 2 – The great desertion from political life 3 – Emergence of the new majority 4 – Political status of the super-rich and underclass 5 – Characteristics of the new majority 6 – Their monopoly of knowledge 7 – But hidden financial knowledge is their need and right 8 – Why the mechanisms of the financial world should be public knowledge

1 – The demise of the left/right political conflict

In grasping the scientific explanation for our present condition, we need to understand the reasons for the breakdown of the democratic process which has sustained political life as a reality for two hundred years. From the time of the French Revolution until approximately 1960, the left/right divide expressed in conflictual terms, the progress of humanity in the developed world.

Today, however, this conflictual process has become no more than a theatrical façade or mere play-acting, and anyone who has kept abreast intelligently with political life, is aware of this fact. But it is a theatrical façade which needs to be kept alive because there is nothing else to replace the illusion. It is a façade which not only deals in facts and figures, but far more significantly, it expresses the entire language of politics. Hence the disappearance of the façade would make politics itself unthinkable. This is because the entire language of politics would be wiped off the map.

Entrapped in such a situation, all politicians within the established order, both locally and nationally, are obliged to become unintentional self-deceivers. They may prefer not to live a lie, but are forced to do so due to the only language, or mode of expression, which is open to them. The only remaining consolation for this collective situation of self-deceit is that politics has been transformed into a game, and the good-natured banter and gentle invective between rivals is seen as symptomatic of the advance of civilisation and good manners rather than as a symptom of degeneration. Nothing in itself is regarded any longer as truly serious, and the apology for this attitude may be explained through relativism or the philosophy of post-modernism. "Principles" or "ideology," or systems of belief, are regarded as no more than a convenient coat or livery of party identification onto which may be stitched any manner of policies or intentions.

Pragmatism, or short-term ideas of the moment in sustaining party credibility is all that matters; and in pragmatism is blindly placed all trust in advancing the progress of humanity or the nation state. In such an irrational environment, and fog of confusion, nations stumble blindly from one blunder to another, and in piling up ill-thought out legislation one on top of the other, they compound their problems.

For almost two centuries, and certainly from the 1840s until 1960 or thereabouts, democratic struggle was predominantly perceived as a conflict between the left and right, or between the Haves and Have-nots, or between those who wanted change and those who wanted to maintain the status quo, for during this period that was the *reality* of political life. This reality was based on the clear division of society into significantly large economic interest groups threatening an explosive situation within society. Such an explosive or revolutionary situation, could only be diverted through the safety valve of the democratic process which formalised the open discussion of differences, whilst slowing down the pace of change.

These interest groups comprised classes which not only defined their separate economic interests – and these are always the defining parameters of class – but also described their cultural attitudes and outlook on the world. Their cultural attitudes were, of course, moulded by and formed unconsciously by their economic interests, but it also needs to be borne in mind that cultural factors served to disguise the harshness, or to morally justify the conflicting economic causes which were pursued. Class struggle or class war cannot be pursued through economic means alone. Such conflict needs the catalyst of cultural factors which are developed in strengthening the solidarity of classes in preparing them for democratic or more explosive forms of struggle.

2 – The great desertion from political life

In this way emerged the proletariat, or propertyless wage-labourers, in their battle with the business and money-owning bourgeoisie. There existed, of course, a lesser or milder struggle between other classes in the pre-industrial age, but here we are only concerned with social movements from the era of the industrial revolution commencing in the mid-18th century.

The emergence of democracy in tandem with class struggle entailed essentially a struggle between ownership and non-ownership in all the aspects in which this may be understood, but such a struggle and governmental democracy *as we have known it* until the present, is only practicable when society is polarised into two or more significant blocks. It is hence essentially a product of modern industrialisation, and this helps explain why democracy is unworkable – if not loathed and met with active hostility – in many non-industrialised countries of the world, both historically and up to the present day.

The attitudes and culture of both the proletariat and the bourgeoisie emerged initially as unintentional influences, but were soon developed consciously both politically in confronting the external world, and internally in strengthening the identity and confidence of those who belonged. As the two cultures grew in sophistication and depth *vis-à-vis* their values and understanding of existence, so too the class struggle became more acute.

It is important to underline the fact that although the so-called working and middle classes may be sub-divided into differing levels with their own attitudes and prejudices, the cultures of the proletariat and the bourgeoisie which emerged in the modern age (i.e. from the time of the Reformation), were unique in world history, and cannot be properly compared with classes of other territories or periods of history. The dominance of Western civilisation tends to hide this fact from Westerners themselves, and has led to widespread misunderstanding throughout the world, especially in recent times and particularly, as reflected through the frequent failures of American foreign policy.

Of most significance, however, is the fact that the existence of these classes (of relatively recent origin) is dependent on the fixity of the economic system. As soon as the economic system changes, so to do the classes, and their relationship with one another. This is something not commonly understood, and perhaps which many might be reluctant to recognise. After all, there is something demeaning to our humanity in the idea that our most cherished attitudes and values should be subject to external forces rather than the innate volition of our own minds. The reality remains that in the larger issues of life we remain the victims of deterministic forces. And here we reach the central argument of this book.

Over the past 200 years, the political democratic system in resolving the left/right divide, has performed its proper function – and performed it well. It has performed it so well that it has brought it almost to completion. This is not to suggest that all political problems have been resolved – quite the contrary, for new and even larger problems confront us in the future. But the democratic system based on the left/right divide is no longer capable of furthering the progress of humanity or nation states. A stage has been reached when the old mechanisms have ceased to work, and unbeknown to our politicians and statesmen and stateswomen, they cannot figure out that the motor of political life in advancing progress has ground to a halt.

Our politicians fail to understand the cause of the crisis since they are looking in the wrong direction. Attempts at meddling with the Constitution or reforming parliament are all doomed to failure. The un-workability of the political system, or expelling hereditary peers are unlikely issues to set us on a better footing. Out politicians would do better to look in the direction of their electors. The key to the problem is that society and the world of work have been transformed out of all recognition over the past 60 years, and consequently, our politicians have been left high and dry in an arid intellectual zone. They are no longer capable of relating with voters, or communicating a message of any sense.

11 – Emergence of the new majority

What, therefore, has occurred? Two contradictory factors have arisen: one offering hope for the future; and the other threatening to destroy prosperity for the majority, and yet with the compensating factor of a new system of democracy on the horizon.

The first concerns the emergence of the heterogeneous middle-middle majority with its potential of mutating into an entirely new class, with characteristics quite different from those of either the proletariat or the bourgeoisie. In the advanced industrial economies in both East and West, in the post-War period, we have experienced a huge surge in the living standards of the majority through the industrial pursuit of consumerism linked to taxation and other policies contributing to greater social justice and a more egalitarian society. A once pyramidal formed society has now been transformed into an egg-shaped society stood on its thicker end. Whilst the smaller minority at the apex represent the super-rich, usually deriving their income from usurious financial activities; that larger minority at the base represents a heterogeneous population of the poor and disadvantaged who have sunk to their existing situation through a broad variety of circumstances from every sector of society. Meanwhile the widely diverse 90%+ majority between these poles are an economic and cultural mix representing a cross-section of the entire population.

The significant factor arising from this revolutionary-scale transformation of society is that it renders a democratic political system of class war impracticable. There are two reasons for this: firstly, because there are not sufficiently large population blocks to engage in battle against one another; and secondly, and equally significant, there are no longer clearly identifiable or sufficiently homogeneous classes willing or capable of engaging in conflict. Class struggle is no longer an option if the cultural factors are absent.

4 – Political status of the super-rich and the underclass

A closer look at the contemporary class situation further helps to elucidate the above points. It will be found that confrontational classes have everywhere – or are everywhere in the process – of withering to extinction. The 2 ½ % at the apex of society are culturally highly heterogeneous and originate from every sector of society, and by no stretch of the imagination represent a political block, since their views are as varied as those found amongst the middle-middle majority.

1 ½ % may be said to comprise the financial rentier class, i.e. self-styled "industrialists," or bankers, brokers, money-lenders, etc., and later we shall demonstrate how their interests are in conflict with those of the rest of the population. But because of their limited number they are incapable of exerting themselves *overtly* as a political force. They are therefore obliged to operate covertly through other political or academic bodies, and of most importance to themselves, through disguising their ends through deceptive economic theories.

The other 1% comprising the super-rich at the apex of society consists of pop and sports stars, TV and film personalities, and a handful of entrepreneurs. Hence the upper classes as a visible or politically overt body are currently insignificant. In emphasising this situation a comparison may be made with their status a hundred years ago. At that time they represented a powerful landowning class linked to the City financial interests of relatively recent created capital

They were a homogeneous class, and the newly rich sought to imitate their betters, and not only did they associate closely at country house parties, etc., in consolidating their interests, but they were visible as a class through their dress, speech, and manners. Above all, they experienced a sense of status and class consciousness which set them above the rest of society. None of these characteristics can be said to exist at the apex of contemporary society anywhere in the modern industrialised world. This is primarily because the forces of democracy have shattered the self-confidence of those throughout every sector of society through taxation and a broad raft of legislation contributing to draw on the brainpower of the masses in maintaining technological progress, and the practical *necessity* for egalitarianism in broadening the base of higher education.

If we turn to the base of contemporary society, we discover a similar situation, i.e., the lack of essential factors contributing to a political class. The underclass may currently be estimated at 7 ½ % of the population, but it does not constitute in any proper sense a proletariat – although in Marxist terms it may be denominated a *Lumpenproletariat.* It constitutes those originating from every sector of society: those who have been impoverished through circumstances beyond their control, or through criminality, alcoholism, or drug addition, etc., the severely disabled or mentally sick, and the unfortunates who have experienced bankruptcy or insolvency through the risks of commerce. The largest sector comprises those population pockets of redundant industries, i.e., the long-term unemployed amongst mining, shipbuilding and other semi- or unskilled manufacturing communities.

The hopelessness and redundant skills of this class ensure their political powerlessness, and their apathy and impotence is expressed through contempt for all political groups. I well remember some years ago, when I and other Labour party members were canvassing for votes in a depressed area with a bad reputation, that this was the only part of town where we received verbal abuse and even the risk of physical assault. In the same town, in leafy suburbs with large villas and spacious gardens, on the contrary, we were often welcomed by the affluent with a social conscience and handed generous donations for the party. That was at a time before New Labour was exposed for the fraud it had always been from the beginning. I relate this story since it illustrates a symptom of the breakdown of the old class political values which had existed at least until the 1960s.

5 – Characteristics of the new majority

In turning to the middle-middle majority we uncover a class, or sector of society, that is more heterogeneous than any other. Not only does it embrace the majority of those who once belonged to – or are descended from – the so-called working or upper classes, but also those with every conceivable opinion, from every religious, racial, and other background. In a sense, at the present time, they do not properly constitute a class in the economic meaning as we have defined it, but they will shortly be forced by a catalyst, as we explain below, which will catapult them into becoming the most prestigious class of the future.

The middle-middle majority are characterised by many of the materialistic values and possessions of the old middle class, whilst also expressing dominating values and attitudes quite different from those of the sector they have replaced. The new majority are not endowed with the class pride and sense of status which marked the bourgeoisie. They neither need fear nor despise the existence of a proletariat which might threaten to overthrow the world as they know it, since that former proletariat is now integrated through possessions, extended rights, and egalitarian circumstances into the middle-middle majority. Of course there still exists that underclass of 7 ½ %, but politically it is powerless, and is merely regarded as problematic and in need of ongoing legislation in alleviating its specific wants.

On the other hand, for reasons elucidated below, the middle-middle majority sense their vulnerability in a dangerous world ruled by administrations incapable of challenging the greatest issues of the age. Whilst on the one hand, as individuals, they are fully prepared to take on the financial and other responsibilities for themselves and their families, and would be loathed to be seen in any way as suppliants of the state; on the other hand, they would choose to view themselves as living in a classless and class-free society.

This latter stems from the need for occupational flexibility; the emergence of numerous skilled occupations (e.g., information technology) without status associations; and the changing status of the older professions, due primarily to their expansion, and consequent loss of aura which they once exerted. For example, solicitors and medical professionals are today so widespread throughout the community, and many of their practitioners may have risen from the "working class" or other one-time possibly disdained minorities, that they no longer dominate society with the exclusive privileges formerly enjoyed in an earlier epoch.

Naturally, earnings vary widely within the middle-middle majority, but it is no longer bourgeois or middle class in the old sense; and likewise, those earning below the average wage are not proletarian or dependent in the old sense for the reason of their responsibility in managing possessions, their materialism, and the diversity of occupations to be found amongst all family groups. Hence the working class solidarity strengthened through shoulder-to-shoulder identical type employment in local communities is for the most part gone forever, partly through computer aided manufacturing (CAM) technologies, leading to the contraction of workforces, and the greater dissemination of specialised but small manufacturing plants, and partly due to a higher percentage of those employed in a broad range of tertiary or service industries. It is in the public sector where the spirit of solidarity is best maintained in contemporary society, e.g., in hospitals and healthcare, and education, but even in these sectors, increasing professional skills brings ever-greater diversification of labour.

6 – Their monopoly of knowledge

The most significant factor about the middle-middle majority, in contrasting it with the entirety of the old class system existing until the 1960s, is that collectively it embodies the monopoly of all knowledge for the control of society and the means of production, distribution, and the means of exchange. This is not to suggest it *exerts* that control, but only that it has the potential for doing so. This stems from a number of reasons, which may be cited as under:-

1. It enjoys a professional and technical educational level never experienced in any previous era;
2. It is more socially and politically informed through the media of its prospects, dangers, and other possibilities of the future; and,
3. Knowledge *per se* is no longer held as the guarded preserve of exclusive elites as it once was.

This is not to say we have yet achieved the open-knowledge society, for we are continually seeking to unlock doors to hidden chambers, but the middle-middle majority are nonetheless pressing all kinds of established bodies to reveal their jealously defended secrets. Knowledge is power, and the implications of this are fully understood by the new majority, and they are demanding their fair share of the exertion of that power. This contrasts sharply with the situation pertaining more than 60 years ago.

In that era of deference, when even BBC interviewers still touched a forelock in addressing premiers and other establishment figures, professional knowledge was jealously guarded as the exclusive preserve of the initiated to which outsiders had no right to intrude. In this way elites were able to retain their power over the majority and conceal abuses through class-based masonic organisations and all kinds of secret or semi-secret bodies, and when challenged over their purposes and mode of activity, they cunningly responded by describing themselves as belonging to "private" associations.

That hidden knowledge of most significance in withholding power from the majority was obviously concerned with the business of government and its convoluted relationship with the financial-industrial establishment. This may sound a strange assertion when applied to such an allegedly "leading" world democracy as Britain, for surely in the name of freedom and in enabling the effective participation of the electorate, we have always sought to educate and explain how government "works." The teaching of constitutional and electoral law, and how it is administered, has always been encouraged. But a knowledge of constitutional law and how it is administered, howsoever carefully studied, tells little about the *actuality* of power as we are all affected through the executive, and even less about the clever manipulation of legislation in leaving the truly powerful well alone.

Even today we know almost nothing about the machinations of small financial elites in manipulating ministers and Administrative class civil servants – except when scandals hit the national headlines as they have recently. And what we do know is merely the tip of the iceberg, and it has revealed government – both local and national – to be often corrupt and rotten to the core. The excuse – or perhaps more correctly the explanation – may be found in the accusation that our rulers are in the pockets of the financial establishment in all their major decision-making, and if this is true, it poses all manner of questions. In any event it costs a dark aspersion on the effectiveness of democracy, and clearly demonstrates that the majority remain the victim of forces against which they have little opportunity to retaliate.

7 – But hidden financial knowledge is their need and right

In an earlier epoch there was always some justification for arbitrary control by elites – but *never* by non-governmental financial elites – and since the majority were not merely uninformed but insufficiently educated, they were not competent to exert any power which really mattered. As a consequence of discontent and revolt, the majority gradually won rights over a period of time, such as the right to vote, but such rights are not necessarily linked to the exertion of power. And indirect power which is passed through the fine filter of representatives and their collective assemblies becomes a very weak brew, and is soon corrupted by other more powerful intervening forces. Nonetheless, in an earlier age of relative ignorance and greater class stratification, such conditions were tolerable for the medium term.

But today, with the emergence of the middle-middle majority, the situation is quite otherwise. In a society which has banished privilege and the idea of deference, and established the groundwork for egalitarian rights through legislation, and ascended a higher level of social consciousness and technical education for all spheres of control, there is now no longer any excuse for withholding knowledge from the majority. And all knowledge affecting the interests of the majority is the right of that majority.

As we shall explain below, the most important sphere of knowledge which it is essential be revealed and passed on to the majority concerns the still hidden secrets of the financial-industrial system and how it operates, for in this is to be found the source of all real power. Without the enjoyment of this power a fully democratic society cannot possibly be realised. The transfer of this knowledge to the majority will be Promethean – i.e., comparable to Prometheus' gift of fire to humanity, and just as such an act incurred the wrath of Zeus, so likewise will it incur the wrath of the usurious financial establishment in their attempts to prevent such a light from reaching humankind.

Money-lending and usury, and to a slightly lesser extent, investment pursued as a profitable activity in itself, have always operated in an environment of partial or total secrecy. They have also usually operated as activities which were apart or separate from the state or government, and often as activities which were barely understood or disdained by the ruling authorities. In the middle ages, for example, there were stringent laws against usury, but in the real world this did not prevent interest rates soaring to levels which would be regarded as intolerable if not inconceivable today. Kings and princes, in their ignorance of the consequences, were often prepared to borrow beyond their means, and when their economies (or thrones) were threatened with collapse, they sometimes turned with savagery on their creditors. In the much more sophisticated world of the 21st century, it is no exaggeration to assert that our political leaders are relatively no less ignorant on financial-industrial matters than their predecessors, the kings and princes who ruled 700 years ago.

And the reason for this ignorance, and the resulting incompetence of governments of all persuasions, is to be found, as we have said, firstly, in the separation between political and financial power; and secondly, in the secrecy of tightly-knit elites in directing financial power. This secrecy is reflected in the pathological sensitivity of the City institutions to any criticism whatsoever, and moreover, their refusal to engage in any kind of discussion on the topic of financial or monetary reform. This is a subject on which I have written at some length, in describing the personal experiences of others as well as myself, in my book, *Social Capitalism in Theory and Practice*. The underlying reason, of course, for this secrecy and sensitivity is that subjective vested interests are being jealously protected. Knowledge is power, and if secret knowledge is revealed to the majority, then that exclusive power is lost

8 – Why the mechanisms of the financial world should be public knowledge

The accumulation of immense riches, or a huge hoard of idle gold and capital, is what the money-lenders or financiers fear to lose through the loss of their exclusive knowledge to the control of wealth. Such power, naturally, is undemocratic and totally unrepresentative – even taking into consideration the charade of the electoral rights of stockholders owning shares in the great corporations, and the nominal right of such insignificant individuals to put a point of view at AGMs.

As financial activity is integral to the welfare of the community, and the latter is integral to the business of government, the majority therefore have a right to the control of financial activity. Such an argument could not always have been maintained in the past. Quite apart from the fact that the middle-middle majority have evolved educationally to fit them to manage the financial sector, the business of government has been greatly extended over the past two centuries. Two hundred years ago the business of government extended little further than raising taxes to maintain law and order, and wage war when the need was seen to arise. In the contemporary world, in both East and West, the business of government through the necessity of maintaining an efficient technological society, has extended to education, employment promotion, health, old age pensions, and many aspects of welfare.

Hence managing all aspects of finance and the money supply has become the *direct* business of us all through the extended role of government, and as the latter is supposedly part of the democratic process, it follows that the business of finance should be made an open activity for the discussion, criticism, and participation of all. It may, of course, be suggested that it is the business of the Chancellor of the Exchequer to fulfil such a role, but ministers of finance are everywhere the victim of circumstances quite beyond their control – besides being ignorant of those essential and hidden mechanisms of the financial-industrial system. A "good" Chancellor of the Exchequer is therefore no more nor less than lucky to hold office during fortunate years, and overnight he is transformed into a "bad" Chancellor due to unforeseen circumstances. The executive discretion of ministers of finance is so minimal as to be insignificant in controlling what *really* matters within the economy.

All this calls for change in a better future. A glance at the opening up of other spheres of hidden knowledge for public inspection over the past 30 years, clearly points to freedoms and rights which have been won. Many exclusive barriers have been knocked down during this brief period, some due to national legislation and some due to EU reforms. This may be found within the spheres of administrative secrecy, education, law, and especially medicine and the medical profession. No person in his right mind would expect to interfere with the highly skilled professional decision-making of the surgeon engaged in a life-saving operation, but today he would expect to be properly informed on what exactly is involved and the expected progress of the treatment.

Now in the financial sphere, the ordinary citizen has a right to expect very much more than this. Not only are financial matters political matters – although as yet they are not widely recognised as such - and hence should be subject to democratic control; but financial and money matters are constantly of permanent interest to every sensible individual, irrespective of his or her place in society, since our lives are always at the mercy of these forces. Therefore the ordinary citizen has a greater right to know all the serpentine mechanisms of the financial-industrial system. And such a right transcends the important but nonetheless subordinate right to openness with regard to civil service secrecy, or that of seeing his medical records, or police files, etc. Financial matters, of course, need to be politicised in raising the awareness of this right, and its significance in safeguarding the material interests of the ordinary citizen, his future, and his family.

CHAPTER 3
Why the political parties are no longer capable of resolving the new issues of our time

" 'There are two ways to conquer and enslave a nation. One is by the sword. The other is by debt' (Pres. John Adams). Conquest by debt can occur so silently and insidiously that the conquered don't even realise they have new masters. On the surface nothing has changed. The country is merely under new management."

E.H. Brown, *The Web of Debt*, Third Millennium Press, Boton Rouge, Louisiana, 2008, p. 47.

1 – Governmental complacency in the face of affluence

Having considered the transformation of society, and how it offers a greater hope for the future, we must now turn to that other contradictory factor, viz., the dangers which threaten to destroy the prosperity of the majority, whilst also eroding the freedom of us all.

It is this factor which will culminate in acting as a catalyst in turning a highly heterogeneous middle-middle majority from an unidentifiable mass of individuals, each with his or her separate interests and perspective of the world, into a dynamic and unified class with a clear political vision and view of the future. It is this new class which will overthrow – or rather transform – the political system, and expose the charade of the left/right divide to the ridicule and disdain it properly deserves.

A superficial glance at the industrialised world as we find it today would hardly present the possibility for such a prediction. On the one hand, the public present such a front of political apathy and retreat into the comfort of their own concerns, as being in no mind to take initiative for change. On the other hand, their irritation with politicians and their parties is such as to put a plague on both their houses by casting negative rather than positive votes. The electorate feel impotent to exert any kind of influence on government, or to stem what they feel is gradual but inevitable economic decline. Statesmen and politicians realise this, and consequently feel there is little urgency to change things for the better. Therefore, they are content to maintain the meaningless pantomime of knockabout politics which achieves little in resolving substantive issues. Both the people and their leaders keep up the pretence that the old game of politics, with the falsity of its out-dated ideologies and discredited ineffective systems, may last forever – without even questioning what may be around the next corner.

In such an intellectual void, all real thought for the future is banished, or sacrificed on the altar of day-to-day pragmatism where the only serious concern is the next election victory. All this is enabled in the wake of relatively high living standards, reasonably benevolent government, and a quiet environment. But the political calm enjoyed in the complacent advanced industrial economies in both East and West is deceptive, and is not unique in the record of world history. It is the quiet before the storm. Five years prior to the French Revolution, for example, no one could have anticipated the turmoil following the unexpected collapse of the financial system, at a time when the rigours of a once-oppressive regime were being relaxed and when a kindly monarch sat on the throne of France. As with most eras of sudden change, not only were events unexpected but they were beyond the control of those seeking to re-direct the policies of the future.

The situation as it exists today in the advanced economies is that the majority are more equal in the face of justice and egalitarian legislation than they have ever been in world history. But this has not been followed by a spirit of stability and contentment. And neither does it follow, as so many assume, that the majority are apolitical. Everywhere there is a feeling of deep anxiety. The political concern of the majority may not be reflected in the membership of parliamentary groups, but it is certainly expressed through the millions who support the many single issue organisations both nationally and worldwide.

2 – The left's repudiation of business values

Two things have occurred which will unify the middle-middle majority in converting it into a distinctive economic class with all the solidarity which that entails. The first is preparatory in alienating it from the old loyalties. The socialism of the left, in realising the transformation of society and the shifting loyalties of their traditional followers, has responded by softening the message in giving it a wider appeal. New Labour has gone so far as to eschew the term "Socialism," or split it into the more distinctive two syllable "Social-ism." New Labour proved to be no more than a short-term stratagem – and is now repudiated by the party. Its failure was due to its intellectual emptiness and ideological poverty, the vacuities of the Third Way, promoted by such academics as Anthony Giddens of the LSE, and the foolish decision to rely on pragmatism in the hope that this alone might maintain its attraction.

The party has succeeded handsomely in disengaging the support of its traditional members through blatantly reversing not merely every socialist principle, but any essential principles in promoting a just or equitable society. This was expressed in candid terms by the MP, Alice Mahon, following her resignation after 60 years membership of the party, in an interview with Neil Clark. She asserted that "Labour is the party of bankers, not workers. The party has lost its soul, and what has replaced it is harsh, American-style politics. ... I was naïve enough to think that when Tony Blair went we would get a change of direction. But it was just wishful thinking. The thing is that Brown really believes in neoliberalism. Things are getting worse in the party, not better, particularly since Peter Mandelson came back. ... Blair was a cuckoo in the Labour nest. New Labour is nothing whatsoever to do with the Labour party."[4]

---

[4] Neil Clark, "The party has lost its soul," *New Statesman*, 27th April 2009.

The journalist, Andrew Gimson, tackles the problem of Labour's unpopularity from another angle, suggesting that a return to old Labour would not be an answer to its woes, since its current approach to the white working class irritates rather than fulfils their wishes. He writes that, "Labour was called into being to represent the working class, yet for many years it has taken working-class support for granted, and today it spends much of its time talking about things that are positively irritating to many of that class. ... It lacks heart and soul because so many traditional Labour supporters have lost all faith in the party as it now exists: bossy, bourgeois, prudish and prissy."[5]

But the real and underlying reason for the left in failing to maintain its credibility as a democratic movement, arose from the inability to outgrow its class-based confrontational stance. No disguise, or changing of policies, or clever spin could conceal the historical fact that its core philosophy necessitated uncompromising confrontation with those who monopolised the power of knowledge and controlled the levers of finance dominating all aspects of existence. The fact that it set itself against the traditional power bases of society, in the conviction they were both malign and oppressive – without exonerating qualities of any kind – inescapably led them to resent and condemn everything that such power represented. In this way the baby was thrown out with the bathwater. It was a stance necessitating such a subjective attitude to a class enemy, that no hope remained for seeing things in their correct perspective – let alone designing constructive alternative policies. In this way the most reasonable and good-natured were forced to see reality through a distorting lens – even when they were aware of this situation and may have attempted to correct their false impressions.

This is not to say that those on the left intentionally sought to deceive through the invention of false arguments and statistics – at least, not in the post-Soviet era. Their greatest sin might have been – and maybe still be – the notion that the end justifies the means, and the dishonesty which springs from this, but little

---

[5] Andrew Gimson, "Conference sketch," *The Daily Telegraph*, 1st October 2009.

more. Parliamentarians of the left in the developed world have, for the most part, sought consciously to be truthful to objective facts in so far as their core beliefs allowed. Whilst those of lesser integrity may have been "economical with the truth" in the cause of what they imagined was a higher purpose, the more circumspect merely cast a blind eye and pleaded ignorance of those vital factors controlling the fate of humankind. These vital factors not merely touched on the technical aspects of the financial-industrial system, but of greater significance, the motivations or human values facilitating the dynamism of business, without which the latter and wealth creation could not flourish in the first place.

Hence the problem of the left led finally to analysing the problem of human or moral values. The badness of the powerful, who oppressed the majority, was not simply to be found in their deeds and purposes, but rather in their thought processes and driving motivation. It is necessary to look at these conflicting sets of values, for although they may rarely be exposed to open discussion, or even subjected to serious thought, they are nonetheless implicit in the aims and actions of parties of both the right and left. These values may be stereotypical and superficial, but they remain *real* in the world of perceptions where blame is cast in explaining motivations condemned as contrary to the social good.

3 – The inescapable essence of business activity

In modern industrialised societies where change is necessarily ever-present, the right may be said to represent the striving of individualism towards acquisition and self-improvement. The urge towards acquisition is no less important than that towards self-improvement in the constructive task of Social Wealth Creation. The activity of business or commerce is always seen as representing the interests of the right, but the only alternative to a society without business is a community reduced to the drudgery of a peasant society, where initiative, inventiveness, and even the arts are kept to a basic level of development. Although such a society was at one time romanticised during the Victorian era, a return to such conditions would be intolerable and inconceivable in the contemporary world. Of course there were many in the 19th century who were appalled by the conditions of the wage-slave worker, and the crass injustice of class divisions, and any alternative may have been imagined as preferable than those existing, but today in the Northern hemisphere we do not live in such a world.

Nonetheless, despite all such changes and material improvements in raising the majority out of a misery they once endured, the left still look askance at business as something distasteful and threatening to the common good. Let us analyse those allegedly unacceptable qualities. They are to be found in the fact that there is always a tension between buyer and seller. There is just no escape from the conflict which arises between the buyer who would pay less and the seller who would charge more – howsoever humane or benevolent the latter might choose to be in negotiating a specific situation. In a marketing situation no absolute or objective value or price can be put on a product or service, although custom or law may place a price on these things. The value of most things is most easily expressed through their price, and this is how most things are exchanged in the everyday commerce of ordinary people.

But just as values fluctuate in the normal course of life, as usually dictated through scarcity, so likewise in a free society, the fixity of prices is impossible, and the cost of a product or service will not only vary from area to area, but even from day to day, due to a broad raft of circumstances. And it is here, in an inescapable negotiating situation, where those on the left will attempt to find a moral flaw in the business process. The seller as the rightful owner, will always have the stronger hand in a bargaining situation. He can hold out the carrot and then withdraw it from the buyer, and it is here where there is room for psychological guile and clever argument, or ingratiating gestures, or enhanced descriptions of the product, or even false suggestions as to other interested buyers.

In such a situation the business person (as vendor) is seen somehow as at worst a bully or at best a poseur, moving constantly within and without the frontiers of deceit in his efforts to close a sale. But then the ordinary citizen, from any sphere of society, is likely to find himself in just such a situation from time to time, and to experience the same feelings and actions described above. And then the buyer, too, can exert his own power, feign disinterest in the product and make gestures of withdrawal. In this way tension is created between both parties to a sale, and in the resulting conflict of negotiation, both may be seen to trick the other with false responses.

4 – The dichotomy of Labour's approach to industry

To those on the left there is something demeaning in such a relationship, for it is seen to corrupt and undermine the integrity of individuals who otherwise would lead a more cooperative or rational existence. It is seen to break the normal transactions of mutual understanding which usually exist in human relationships. Such perceptions, however, lead to an entirely false view of morality. The process of business in resolving a difficult sales or other situation does not in reality demean or corrupt, but rather temporarily move the consciousness of those involved into an unknown area. The conclusion of such situations is always unknown – as otherwise there would be no need for such discussion in the first place – and so consequently, unconscious and irrational forces are inevitably evoked, and the outcome is that the participants act in a way they had not originally anticipated.

The moral justification for every such business episode is that finally the outcome is agreed between the two parties and is mutually agreeable. If dissatisfaction is later felt by one partly to a deal, then this only gives rise to self-blame for failing to comprehend all the aspects in the exchange. None of the above is intended to justify corrupt or deceitful modes of business, or what I have elsewhere described as Unsocial Wealth Creation, and these I shall touch upon later in this book. The above refers only to open modes of business between honest and consenting individuals.

An extreme example of the socialist attitude to monetary relationships, typical of certain sectors of society, may be illustrated by the experiences of a friend who took in an unemployed youth as a lodger, to be confronted a fortnight later by the declaration that no more rent would be paid until the landlord was ordered by the authorities to reduce the amount. The youth had been to Social Services who said they would act for the young man. The weeks passed and my friend received not a penny in return.

When he then gently approached his lodger on the matter, the latter responded violently by saying he was a socialist and didn't believe in money, and that "property was theft" and should be held in common by all, and that as his landlord was a "Christian and a churchgoer," he should follow the "commandments of his Lord," by supporting the poor and downtrodden. When the landlord responded by evicting the tenant, he was prosecuted through the aid of Social Services, but fortunately, in view of all the circumstances, the court ruled there was no case to answer. There is here something very wrong with the moral values of society if such religious ideas may be evoked against contractual obligations, or to justify what could lead to an anarchic situation.

If the above sounds in any way exceptional, the attitude of those on the left to business activity – and especially amongst politicians – generally remains deeply negative. During many years of active membership within the Labour party, as a businessman, I have often personally encountered such prejudice. At gatherings and conferences I was always initially met with friendly gestures, but as soon as my occupation was known, faces fell and I was made to feel unwelcome. I was probably thought to be an academic or doctor, or one of the many management consultants feeding off the NHS, but as soon as it was revealed I was in industry – promoting UK-based employment – I felt I was henceforth regarded as a political pariah to be avoided.

On no occasion was I ever reproached for being in industry, but sometimes silence or body language speaks volumes, when words are deceptively used to conceal what is really felt or meant. In political life (across the spectrum) there are too many thoughts and issues which may never be exposed to open expression. Self-censorship may be the worst of all in suppressing opinion and the exchange of knowledge.

Few responsible parliamentarians on the left would dare express their disdain for business in explicit terms. Instead, in their quiet contempt, they choose to raise a mental barrier against comprehending business with regard to its practical or ethical implications. In my book, *The People's Capitalism*, I have described this as the missing "gene" of socialism. In this way they feel they best ensure defending the interests of the oppressed and disadvantaged.

But such a stance leads the parliamentary left into compounding all their problems, for in the cause of good pragmatic electioneering to win over "middle England," they are forced to proclaim themselves as the standard bearers of business. The outcome is that instead of setting about the reform of the financial-industrial system, they have taken capitalism as they find it, and rather than promoting UK employment-giving activity, they have advanced the worst aspects of business. That is, they have befriended usurers and leading City moguls, and continued to push Thatcherite policies to further limits. This has led to increasing de-industrialisation, and inevitably and most recently, to pushing up unemployment.

The schizophrenic attitude of the Labour party leadership could not be better illustrated than by citing personal experiences which arose through my membership of the Labour Finance and Industry Group, comprising a body of leading industrialists advising the front bench. Shortly before Tony Blair was elected to the premiership, he attended a function of the LFIG at the Reform club. On entering the library, in which the function was held, he betrayed a certain diffidence, as if suddenly finding himself amongst a den of thieves. To reassure him, Dr. Peter Slowe, the Secretary of the Group, who was acting as host, exclaimed (to some laughter), "Don't be afraid, Tony, we're all friends here – we're all signed up members of the Labour party."

The LFIG included a number of industrialists, bankers, and even stockbrokers with radical ideas for financial reform, and were keen to ensure their invaluable contributions reached the ear of the party. Sub-committees were formed and useful discussion and much research was undertaken in advancing the cause of the movement. When, however, Labour was elected to power, these radical groups were sidestepped, and those who had always upheld the usurious economy moved ahead in taking over the control of the association.

This unprincipled attitude to business is possibly derived from ignorance rather than guile – although greed does play a part. In the words of Ross Clark, "this Labour government has become an even greater friend of shysters than its earlier Harold Wilson manifestation. Labour has such a blind spot regarding business that it simply cannot distinguish between where business ends and racketeering begins. It is as if the whole world of profit-seeking is so foreign to Gordon Brown and his companions that they have been unable to recognise the concept of making an honest buck.

"This certainly applied to the banks, where Mr. Brown was bamboozled by the money cascading into his Treasury. His government, let us never forget, took a 40% cut in all the bonuses paid: the greed of the financiers themselves was matched by a greed, by government, for the tax haul. This was a no-questions-asked kind of greed, where Mr. Brown did not wonder whether money was being made by fair or foul means, as long as it paid for his public services."[6]

This illustrates clearly the futility of placing any hope of the parliamentary left in advocating intelligent or effective reforms for our financial-industrial infrastructure. The Labour party, as well as other parliamentary movements of the left worldwide, have shamelessly pursued the irresponsible policies

---

[6] Ross Clark, "We have become a nation of shysters," *The Spectator*, 17th October 2009.

of the debt-creating casino economy in the wake of the international penetration of American financial practices over the past twenty years.

The impotence of the Labour party, for example, to even attempt implementing superficial legislation in reining in the City and corrupt bankers, following the catastrophic crash in 2008, was pointed out in a savage piece of journalism by Rod Liddle about a year later, when he wrote, "Nothing has changed. The economic crisis of last year is still seeing people put out of work – poor people, natch – but the next boom is being feverishly pumped up right now, on the same grounds as before. Nothing has changed – all that stuff about greater regulation, prudence, stability, financial propriety and a cap on extravagant bonuses? Bankers wandering around looking hurt and contrite and wondering if they should maybe open a donkey sanctuary in Suffolk instead of bankrupting the nation?

"You're joking – nobody in the City is taking the slightest notice and they never have. That's all 'neo-socialist claptrap,' as Boris Johnson, London's Conservative mayor, eloquently put it. In those clamorous City wine bars the champers is already on ice because it's business as usual – except this time even more so and, remarkably, overseen by the same people who brought us to financial ruin."[7] This is not only clear evidence of the government's incompetence to safeguard majority needs, but the necessity for a new political order to rid the country of endemic financial skulduggery.

5 – How the class-based perspective depresses standards

What, therefore, are the values of the left – or what remains of them? At core they entail bureaucratic values, i.e., the reduction of decision-making within a supposedly rational or Weberian framework of collective cooperation. In the emphasis on protecting the less advantaged, it is assumed that the *conditions* for their advancement should be put on a different

---

[7] Rod Liddle, "The bankers haven't learned that greed is good ... for nothing," *The Sunday Times*, 4th October 2009.

basis from those alleged to be their oppressors. This is expressed through the assumption of irreconcilable interests between the classes, and hence is used to justify class struggle as a political weapon. But the assumption that the disadvantaged should be placed in a different situation from the rest of the population, usually through preferential legislation or negative discrimination against those of average or higher ability, achieves little in its purpose of integration whilst diminishing overall higher aspirations and standards.

Such policies are always patronising in the sense that normal standards are pushed aside in making room for those of lower ability (and possibly lesser initiative), as justified through their pecuniary situation. And patronage, irrespective of the donor, is always resented. This critique is applied, it should be noted, in referring to the *general population* as defined in excluding those with physical or mental disabilities. The latter, on grounds of equity and justice, it is argued, should always be granted special dispensation in every attempt to raise them to equality with the more fortunate. But in a truly egalitarian society of the *general population*, there is no justification for legislation deferring to the cultural prejudices of class if this acts as a threat to undermining recognised standards, or the quality aspirations of upward mobility. This is the problem of the mindset of the left.

The answer to the problem of the disadvantaged can only be found in transforming the educational system, particularly with regard to instilling values and aspirations, and ensuring that all are obliged to meet those higher standards necessary in maintaining an efficient industrial society. In meeting the needs of an egalitarian society, education should be standardised, but in such a way as to aspire to the traditional ideals of Rugby and Eton rather than of Bermondsey or Bow. In reality, of course, a middle way must be met between the two extremes. In other words, a common mindset must be created through a reformed educational system, whereby the youth of Stepney or Whitechapel are taught to see the world and share the same ideals and aspirations as those in Richmond or Highgate. This is the route to true equality and social justice, for a stable and unified society can never be achieved through the divisive policies of class war.

6 – Bye-passing the business mindset undermines the economy

An aspect of left-wing collectivism, which is no less malign than its call for class divisiveness, is its attempt to resolve the inequity of maldistribution through purely rational means, i.e., through legislation which bye-passes the business process. The panacea of socialist economic policies carried to their logical conclusion have now, of course, been totally discredited worldwide following the collapse of the Soviet bloc, but the blind spot of the left in understanding and appreciating the essence of the business dynamic, as we have noted above, still remains. The idea of competition, and the striving of the individual in pursuing his own interests, clashes entirely with the ideals of the left.

Whilst striving for the collective ideal is interpreted as moral, striving for personal and individual ends is regarded as morally questionable and certainly as selfish. In making judgements in the real world it is sometimes necessary to refer to the measuring rod of the Aristotelian golden mean, and whilst extreme acquisitiveness and self-centredness is certainly reprehensible, at the other end of the spectrum, carelessness of one's interests or reckless altruism is almost equally so. True virtue demands a middle course, and in this instance, it calls for self-regard within the moral constraints of society in pursuing one's own best interests.

The ultimate critique of left wing values is not only that they unintentionally but inevitably restrict the freedom of the individual, and all this means in preventing the full development of the personality and intellectual potential; but that they hold back social and technological progress. The collapse of the Soviet Union demonstrates clearly the fallibility of collective rationalism pushed to its logical conclusion in totalitarianism, and the inability of myopic dictatorship confronting the technological creativeness of a relatively free society in better advancing the material interests of the majority. The weakness of the former model stems primarily from its failure to promote competition and diversity in commerce and all spheres of creativity, from whence the progress of humankind owes its origin.

7 – Economic policies of the right have been no less disastrous

It might be thought that the above contributes to the defence of the right – particularly with regard to financial-industrial questions in view of the notorious fact of socialism's missing "gene" – but nothing could be further from the truth. The recent history of the past 30 years has demonstrated that the parties of the right have been as bad – or even worse – in their pursuit of economic policies damaging the interests of the majority, than those on the left. It would be difficult to imagine a more damaging regime that that of Margaret Thatcher – arguably the worst ruler this country has had to endure since the reign of King John. And judging by a recent survey of prospective first-time Tory MPs,[8] the future looks little more promising. Although David Cameron and his leadership are committed to a more humane one-nation Conservatism, apparently 90% of first-time prospective MPs are declared Thatcherites, who unanimously concluded she was the "best peace time Tory premier" of the 20th century. Such views reflect an atrocious ignorance of recent economic history, and a state of denial with regard to the causes of both personal and public debt. If the Conservative party is unable to pick a better team than these, then it really has been reduced to scraping the bottom of the intelligence barrel.

The rise of the casino economy, following in the wake of innovative American financial methods and products assuring a "quick buck," rapidly undermined the employment-giving

---

[8]   Undertaken by the *Today* programme on BBC Radio 4, on 8th October 2009.

productive base of Britain, and at a later stage, of many other countries. The recent quip by that percipient political thinker and friend of presidents, Gore Vidal, that Britain "isn't a country, it's an American aircraft carrier,"[9] was only made possible through the appalling economic policies of Margaret Thatcher which remain with us until this day. It was hardly recognised at the time that money-creation is *not* wealth creation, or alternatively, it may be described as Unsocial Wealth Creation. It is true that Thatcher was elected into power to confront the destructive misdeeds of trades union power, but the central argument of this book is that raising one opposite against another does nothing to resolve underlying substantive issues. Ding-dong politics has all the idiocy of the cockpit, and only produces resentment and blood-letting – or it does during the present advanced stage of democratic evolutionary progress.

Thatcherism entailed an orgy of money making money, without accompanying social benefits, and whilst the stock market shot through the roof in rewarding an army of satisfied rentiers, factories were everywhere going into liquidation and millions lost their jobs. Whilst the short-term benefits may have buried the evidence of long-term ruin which was developing below the surface, the problems of the dispossessed, the insolvent, and the unemployed were dismissed as irrelevant to the economic purposes of the time. In this way blatant usury was placed on a pedestal – the government remaining oblivious to the immorality and ruinous consequences of usurious activity of any kind. An in-depth analysis of Thatcherite or Neo-liberal economic policies will be found in my book, *Social Capitalism in Theory and Practice.*

If the above describes the practical work of the right in recent times, it is necessary to turn to their core beliefs that have brought these about. Whilst on the one hand the right support the freedom of the individual, which in itself is praiseworthy, when this is then linked to the philosophy of laissez-faire, it becomes immediately problematical. This is because laissez-

---

[9] In an interview with Johann Hari, "Gore Vidal's United States of Fury," *The Independent* (Life section), 7th October 2009.

faire (or letting things be) is a social and not an individual activity which impacts in unanticipated and harmful ways on significant sectors of the community if not accompanied by desirable intervention. Free trade is vital for the health of commerce, but this too calls for definition in discriminating between Social and Unsocial forms of wealth creation.

The ideology of the parliamentary right in modern industrialised societies is therefore based on trust in Adam Smith's concept of the "invisible Hand," and this in turn is used to justify every development of the capitalist process, including the worst aspects of usury which undermine the home-based productivity of nation states. Adam Smith is projected as the economic guru of the right, but this entails a gross distortion of his economic theories, for as a moral philosopher he already anticipated the abuses of free-wheeling capitalism in damaging the interests of the employed.

8 – Social versus Unsocial capitalism

In the nonsensical ding-dong of political life, socialism responded by condemning *all* forms of capitalism in throwing out the baby with the bathwater, and in a former epoch in the pre-1980s, in discussion with Labour party members and trade unionists, it was impossible to get them to analyse capitalism so that benign and malign aspects could be clearly differentiated. The situation changed in the later 80s and 90s, and particularly after John Monks became the General Secretary of the TUC when the concept of "partnership" was wisely adopted, but even then, the unions held back from seizing the opportunity they might have taken. I had several meetings with John Monks whom I admired, but I felt he was nonetheless restrained by hardliners in the trades union movement.

I was the first person to differentiate clearly between benign or Productive capitalism as against malign or Rentier capitalism with the publication of my pamphlet, *New Life For British Industry*, which was promoted by Sir Peter Parker, and financed by the leading industrialist advocating changes to

Company law, George Goyder. The pamphlet was launched at the SDP's Conference at Torquay in September 1985, and some years later the same ideas were independently launched by the French economist, Michel Albert, using a different terminology, with the publication of his book, *Capitalism Against Capitalism*, in Paris in 1993. Rather than the type-descriptive terms, which I had chosen, he opted for the geographical terms of Neo-American capitalism versus the Rhine-mode of capitalism – the latter to include the Far East Tigers.

This political philosophy which I was eventually to label, *Social Capitalism*, was and still remains too problematical for the parliamentary parties of the left or right, or even of the centre, to dare to adopt. This is primarily because it undermines the cornerstone of Punch and Judy politics, and if successful, would eventually bring the system crashing down. Hence, through the needs of expediency and in protecting the careers of our representatives, political life remains locked into a situation from where it is impossible to progress either intellectually or in practical terms. I have not touched on the role of the centre parties, in whom originally I had most hope, since despite their positioning within the left/right spectrum, and the greater sanity which this would seem to present, they offer no deciding way out of our puzzling situation. There are four reasons for this:-

1. They represent a mishmash of ideas from the other two parties;
2. They are not sufficiently committed to either the interests of capital or labour to give sufficient authority or thought to resolving these most important issues of all;
3. Their opportunism concentrates their energies on cleverly balancing conflicting forces; and most significantly,
4. Their distance from power is insufficient to motivate their intellectual energies towards the creation of a genuinely new political outlook in meeting the real needs of the future.

CHAPTER 4
How corporations have absorbed governments worldwide and neutered democracy

"Markets seldom shape individual's sense of their own identity, organisations do."

Francis Fukuyama, *State Building* Profile Books, 2004, p. 41.

1 – People power through the nation state 2 – Insensitivity of US internationalism 3 – Internationalism of the left 4 – The origins of globalisation 5 – The debt-fuelled economy and widespread dispossession 6 – Dispossession equals democratic disempowerment 7 – Unsocial Wealth Creation in practice 8 – How consumers lose out to the multiples 9 – How corporate power homogenises taste and annihilates individuality

1 – People power through the nation state

Having described the emergence of the new middle-middle majority, and the failure of the existing party political system to hold its allegiance, we must now examine the socio-economic circumstances of this majority, and how these will act as a catalyst for change.

Freedom, democracy, social justice and equity, in all their aspects, are not only dependent on the collective power of the community expressed through government, but on government which is universal or all-powerful. Such a declaration may sound contradictory, or suggest the existence of internal contradictions, since most people sense that *powerful* government suggests an excess of top-down authority or unwarranted authority which interferes with every aspect of life. The phrase all-powerful government is even suggestive of totalitarianism.

But here we are arguing for the opposite of such a tendency. We are arguing that all-powerful government is essential in defending freedom and our rights. Government needs to be all-powerful in preventing the growth of other forces in society, which through their serpentine and impenetrable influence threaten our material well-being, and eventually eat away the foundations of governmental power without our leaders being fully aware of the fact. Hence we understand government, or the state, to mean the representative body intended to express the will of the people through electoral or other processes such as the referenda or plebiscite. If government fails to satisfy the needs or transmit the will of the people, it deservedly loses its authority and respect over those whom it governs.

History has demonstrated that hitherto, the only large-scale political territorial structure which people trust, and in which they feel a proper connectedness, irrespective of whether their society is democratic or otherwise, is the nation state. That is, federations or other supra-national entities have not as yet succeeded in achieving the complete participation, trust, or loyalty of the ordinary citizen. Because of 20th century history in the Western world, and the horrific conflicts which have arisen amongst European states, it is unfashionable to defend nationalism or the nation state. But the history of the last 50 years of the previous century, and the ongoing worldwide crisis of the 21st, should amply demonstrate that national feelings and rights are everywhere of paramount significance. It should also be noted there is only one cause of terrorism in the contemporary world, and that is the failure to recognise the social injustice against those attempting to exert their political rights as oppressed national minorities.

Nationality may be defined as nothing more nor less than cultural identity, and everything through which an individual expresses his beliefs, hopes, and aspirations. This not only includes language, customs, religion, the arts and music, but also concepts on social organisation and government. These are things which are little understood in the Western world, and of which those on the far right and the left have little understanding. The Neo-liberal right and the socialist left have always been irresponsible advocates of a *destructive* internationalism.

2 – Insensitivity of US internationalism

American foreign policy since the 1960s, for example, has both in the first and Third worlds been grossly insensitive and catastrophic, and wherever she has intervened, either diplomatically or militarily, she has worsened the situation in leaving trails of conflict and bloodshed, where previously there was a greater modicum of peace and harmony. The prime vice of America is her arrogance, and the self-delusion that her people are politically the best endowed on the planet, when in reality they tend towards philistine values, and are amongst the least well-governed of any in the advanced industrial world. Their greatest delusion stems from the conviction that their form of democracy is an ideal paradigm which they feel morally obliged to propagate and establish throughout the four corners of the globe.

In my book, *Freedom From America*, I have clearly shown that America is not correctly a democracy, but rather a plutocracy, and that consequently it would be difficult to achieve a just or equitable government under such an administrative system. But worse than that, as far as many Third world peoples are concerned, her rulers are so ill-informed on matters of social science *visa-à-vis* the political-cultural conditions of other territories, as to imagine her system of democracy could be enforced on them, even allowing that such a form of government was practicable in the circumstances. Furthermore, Americans find it hard to comprehend how anyone would wish to resist the "alluring benefits" of her political institutions. Who in the world can live without McDonalds, Mickey mouse, Coca-Cola – or even a proper health service? And even less does she understand there are tribal and developing countries in the world which loathe the very concept of democracy, and would – and do resort to extreme methods in preventing its adoption.

The truth, of course, is that democracy can only be imparted to those peoples reaching a sufficiently high level of education, and this usually means to industrially advanced economies. In fairness to America's political elite, it has to be acknowledged that European powers in too hurriedly shedding their colonial responsibilities have been equally over-optimistic in their expectations with regards to the democratisation of former territories which quickly mutated into oppressive dictatorships. It has to be borne in mind that even in the culturally and industrially developed countries of Western Europe, it was some time, and over a series of stages, before the franchise was made to include entire populations. If the British government had been so foolish, for example, as to extend the franchise to the entire population in 1832, at the time of the great Reform Bill, the country and her greater prospects might have been seriously compromised some 15 years later during the widespread revolutions of 1848. How then, in the light of this, could any *practical* good be expected to result from granting universal franchise to peoples whose level of civilisation was well below that of Europe in the first third of the 19th century?

Although democracy was granted as a right without pre-conditions to former colonial territories in the post-War period, the recognition of that purely abstract right failed to consider both the practicalities of politics and the material welfare of their peoples. Although little is written about the question of de-colonisation (which was partially driven through the misguided policies of American statesmen) during my travel throughout the world, I have been confronted on many occasions by Commonwealth citizens who bemoaned the British withdrawal from their countries as irresponsible and catastrophic to their peoples. Unbeknown to the British left there are possibly more British patriots in the developing territories of the Commonwealth than throughout the entire United Kingdom.

The internationalism of America may indeed be idealistically inspired through her own political vision, but it should be remembered she has financially benefited from every successful intervention. She may have played her laudable game in condemning and scheming for the diminution of European power, but hypocritically, she then advertised the notion of benevolent lending and investment to the Third world, before throwing herself into a programme of financial imperialism which far exceeded anything undertaken by the older nations in an earlier era. The given reason for the insensitivity of America's particular brand of internationalism, and as to why it generates such resentment and hatred globally, stems from her identifying American patriotism and vision of the world with the concept of internationalism in such a way that the two are inseparably linked. This simply reflects a blindness which refuses to acknowledge the value or social significance of different cultures.

3 – Internationalism of the left

In turning to the internationalism of the left, this was inspired by two factors, the first of which shares an affinity with American internationalism: viz. that all humanity is at root identical in sharing the same needs and aspirations. This is a blunt view of humanity, firstly, because needs and aspirations call for definition, and are then highly debatable – and in any case they differ widely; and secondly, because such an abstract concept in practice too easily tends to ignore cultural and historical differences which need always to be respected in political life. With regard to needs and aspirations, for example, clearly the views of America and the Soviet Union were poles apart during the Cold War period, although both proclaimed the international ideal in their different ways.

The second factor of the left's internationalism stems from its ideological repudiation of nationalism, as a force which through the capitalist process gives rise to conflict between peoples, and the evils of war. This was perhaps most famously expressed through Lenin's pamphlet, *Imperialism, The Highest Stage of Capitalism*. The argument may certainly have been valid until the Second World War and beyond, but as we explain below, the world now faces a new possibility with the promise of an economic system ensuring international stability and greater friendship amongst peoples.

In the Western world, the left has been little less insensitive to national cultures than has America due to the determination in planting socialism as a priority above other factors. In Eastern Europe, on the other hand, during a particular period, this insensitivity towards cultural groups took a different turn. In 1937 the population of the Soviet Union, for example, were obliged to complete a questionnaire, innocent enough on the surface, as to national origins. The outcome of this was that millions of non-Russians in that vast empire were arrested and transported to Siberian labour camps, and those few who were not shot, or did not die of malnutrition or exposure, were allowed to return to their desolated homelands many decades later.

In the 21st century we live in a world where the forces of internationalism have never been so powerful or so malign in oppressing peoples in both the advanced and developing economies. Never in history have the economic and cultural aspirations of nations been less regarded than they are today. This has occurred through the rise of the globalised economy during the past two decades; in undermining the self-sustainability of nation states; in promoting de-industrialisation and conditions for massive unemployment in many parts of the world; and not least, in unnecessarily exacerbating the spoliations of the environment and global warming almost everywhere. In political terms, all aspects of internationalism are actively promoted by the right in furthering global or rentier capitalism; whilst the parliamentary left accept globalisation as a *fait accompli* which is futile to resist.

4 – The origins of globalisation

A false palliative offered in attempting to alleviate the seeming gravity of globalisation is that it has always existed through the consequences of international trade, and that the one is simply a natural growth from the other. An examination of the facts, however, demonstrates that globalisation is something quite new in the way it touches on the material interests of peoples and the autonomy of nation states. International trade was formerly conducted under the auspices of new states, or federations, or trading blocs, and admittedly under the powerful guiding hand of gold merchants or financial and banking corporations which were separate from the state, but nonetheless were usually associated with national interests.

Wars, unfortunately, were often brought about through the breakdown of such trading relationships, or through attempts to correct imbalances of power between competing states. In the post-Napoleonic era a quantum leap occurred with the rise of the Rothschilds as an international financial force in the Western world, for although the close family network settled its relatives as *nationals* in leading capitals, they engaged firstly, in loans on a scale which had never been reached before; secondly, in transactions which were truly international in the sense of benefiting the firm in far transcending the mere interests of particular governments; and thirdly, in ensuring the success of the above, in conducting their business with a degree of secrecy and raft of precautions rarely undertaken by previous lending houses.

The sophistication or skill of the Rothschilds, shortly to be followed by the activities of similar families throughout Europe and America, could be taken as the first step of financial-industrial systems in a gradual but unseen chasm to be opened between the underlying interests of the state versus those of independent economic forces unaccountable to any territorial authority. The financial internationalism of these powerful closely-knit family concerns did little, if anything, to avert the onset of catastrophic conflict on a scale never witnessed in previous epochs – and probably helped to promote them through financing huge war machines with unlimited credit.

The next quantum leap was to occur in the decades following the Second World War, when with the strength of the dollar, new financial products and extortionate modes of funding were invented at a hectic pace in meeting the challenges of a world ruined by war and impoverished by debt. When the Bretton Woods institutions of the World Bank and the

International Monetary Fund were founded in the immediate post-War period, in a flurry of good intentions, no one suspected at the time that these were anything less than philanthropic bodies. Their existence may have been initiated by politicians, academics and civil servants with benevolent intentions, but as their operation was to be dependent on bankers and financial corporations, they quickly mutated into usurious institutions which eventually proved ruinous to Third world territories. In using the term usury, it should be noted that this is intended in its modern sense, i.e. the charging of *excessive* interest, and not interest *per se,* as the term is still used amongst those with certain monetarist theories.

5 – The debt-fuelled economy and widespread dispossession

Meanwhile, Neo-American or Rentier capitalism was to embark on the greatest programme of dispossession the world had ever witnessed, first within her own borders, later in Britain, and finally, from the late 1980s and 90s onwards, throughout Europe – including the Russian federation – and many other countries around the globe. This was initially to take the form of dispossession in the commercial field through corporate buy-outs or the amalgamation of enterprises, and so as independents or sole proprietorships were increasingly put out of business, giant conglomerates became ever larger and more powerful in taking over the control of populations in many aspects of their lives.

Later, a similar process was to accelerate dispossession in the domestic sector through mortgage companies raising their interest rates to extortionate levels. In Britain home ownership percentages boomed in the Thatcherite era, enabled through lending policies pushed onto an unwary public by the banks, with no indication as to the dangerous possibility of fluctuating interest rates. The deceptive political cry of "Home ownership" was proclaimed as the new freedom. But in the first decade of the 21st century, worse was to follow in America, for whilst in Britain there existed some protective legislation with regard to the interest rate limits of lending institutions, in America there was none. Consequently, overnight, rates soared, followed quickly by the raids of bailiffs in evicting occupants into the street without the obligation of issuing reasonable notices for such arbitrary and violent action.

The economic consequences of usurious mortgage lending in both America and Britain, and elsewhere (apart from triggering the major financial crisis of 2007-2008) was not home ownership but eventual dispossession, or the reduction of home owners to the status of tenants paying extortionate rents. But worse was the dramatic surge of property values, whereby the younger generation, across all economic sectors of the community, apart only from the super-rich, were placed in the invidious situation of inability to get onto the lowest rung of the property ladder. The economic and social consequences of this have been widespread, forcing adult children to remain in the parental home for longer than they would wish; delaying childbirth or marriage beyond the biologically desirable period, which in turn has led to costly fertility treatment; and finally, to the collapse of the birth rate (particularly amongst the better educated sectors of the population) throughout the Western world and the Confucian peoples of the Far East. All this, of course, leads to other unfortunate consequences for nation states, arising from social conflict and widespread divorce, maladjusted children, domestic violence, higher crime rates, etc.

6 – Dispossession equals democratic disempowerment

The longer term political consequences of this entail a threat to social progress and even to the ideals of civilisation as we know it. The juggernaut of transnational, global, or Rentier capitalism, with its accumulation of the ownership and control of capital into ever fewer hands, is also a process of the accelerating disempowerment of the majority. Neither the freedom of the individual nor a working democracy can be said to exist where the majority are deprived of owning and controlling the means of production, distribution, and the means of exchange. In the industrialised world today democracy has been reduced to a pretence or a meaningless charade. The cause of this has arisen through the disempowerment of national states in those matters of *most* importance to the majority, i.e., economic policy; and it is made most evident through the disillusion of electorates and everywhere the collapse of party memberships.

This process of universal disempowerment might not at first be clearly evident to the ordinary citizen. For example, a visit to any industrial estate involved in manufacturing, metal bashing, or other similar activities, in any part of the country might deceptively convey the impression of a healthy independent sector. This would be conveyed through the variety of logos and company names betraying no sign of corporate takeover. But anyone who actually visits such companies, and talks with their chief executive officers, as I have done in the course of my business career, is soon disabused of any such illusion. He will generally discover that 90% of those seemingly independent firms are parts of groups, and that they in turn may belong to larger conglomerates. As corporate business is not keen to advertise the ubiquity of its power, and as likewise, formerly independent proprietors seek to retain their distinctive identities for as long as they can, they are in no hurry to change their outward appearance.

With regard to those who are obliged to pay bills for gas, electricity – or even water, and wonder why charges are ever rising, they might not do better than look into the ownership of these giant utilities. If they do, they will often find that their supplier is foreign owned – usually situated in France or Germany. The possibilities of blackmail in some unknown future are therefore horrific, or more probably, and less dramatic are the possibility of fuel crises for which no one is to blame, but the outcome of which would entail the sacrifice of supplies to Britain in maintaining essential services to the Continental suppliers. This of course is an imperative argument for every nation state to both *own* and *maintain* all power supplies for its own survival.

Anyone who compares the average high street of today with that of twenty years ago will, however, at once recognise its dramatic change. Gone is the predominance of independence business, to be replaced by chains, multiples, or franchises, together with an excess of building societies which have mutated into banks, alongside a variety of other financial enterprises. Some may respond to such changes by exclaiming, "but what does it matter if business ownership is falling into ever fewer ownership sectors if living standards continue to rise, and if those who are dispossessed continue to be paid salaries comparable to their previous status as proprietors? And, anyway, aren't such trends the evidence of inevitable progress?"

The answer to the second question is a firm No, for the reasons explained below. The answer to the first question is that it matters a great deal if ownership is constantly whittled away. The fact that living standards continue to rise – or have continued to rise over the past six decades up until the present point in time – is to be credited to the development of technology linked to consumerism, and not to the Rentier economy which is now increasingly dominating the countries of the world. Or looked at from another angle, rising living standards have been accountable to the easy availability of credit at high interest, and to a ballooning cash economy which may explode overnight. Usury linked to short-termism is a dangerous mixture, and no recipe for a sound economy.

A comparison between the Productive economies of Continental Europe and the Far East, as opposed to the Rentier economies of America, Britain, and most of the developing world, will in fact reveal that over the greater part of this 60-year period, it is in the former where living standards have risen to a far greater degree. The Productive economy is not typified by the polarisation of ownership and the speculative acquisitiveness of smaller enterprises by larger with the inevitable widening divide between rich and poor.

7 – Unsocial Wealth Creation in practice

The accelerating decline of business ownership, as we are now experiencing, spells disaster on many fronts, and is already undermining the material welfare of the majority, not so much according to economic status in society as according to generational factors irrespective of financial standing. When companies are taken over and their proprietors are turned into employees, they may still retain their titles as Chief Executive Officers, but despite the retention of these external formalities as a sop to their self-esteem, their former position is totally transformed. In all really significant decision-making they are reduced to a powerless situation. For example, they are at once made answerable to a higher financial authority.

Whilst the rationale of their business was formerly the maximisation of market share or product innovation (both of which are beneficial to consumers and the broader community); the first priority is now the maximisation of shareholders' profits, and this may lead to changes in every department of an enterprise. Downsizing and the renovation rather than the replacement of machinery is undertaken not so much for economic reasons as maximising stockholders' dividends. The management vision of the company is transferred from a marketing or engineering aspect to a purely accountancy aspect. The company no longer has the Social purpose or producing widgets for a demanding public, but the Unsocial purpose of exclusively satisfying investors' interests. The latter is not in itself reprehensible (for investors deserve and should be paid their just returns), but such a transformation in a company's purpose leads to its losing its true role as an effective manufacturer and supplier.

With the loss of its true vision it eventually becomes incapable of maintaining its place in the market. This stems from the fact that the new corporate owners are merely accountants with no interest in productivity beyond the speculative potential of an enterprise in money creation for its own sake. If necessary the business is sold for the value of the land, for far more capital may be rapidly raised through property developers than could ever be made through the productivity of labour. It is this which explains the relative decline of industry in Britain, America, and elsewhere in the post-War period, rather than the hoary old excuse of price competition from cheaper labour economies. This is partly demonstrated by the fact that during the greater part of the post-War period, such Productive economies as Finland, Sweden, or Switzerland, with stronger currencies and higher exchange rates than our own, have nonetheless succeeded in maintaining the strength of their industrial sectors through greater innovation and more efficient marketing.

The managing directors of independents, who are then taken over by corporations, whilst retaining their nominal positions, are soon reduced to a shadow of their former selves. This is because policy decisions dictated from above contradict every truth they learned during their working lives. Marketing and quality decisions are always subordinated to those of earning the quick buck, and wherever money can be made out of money, the practical aspects of the core purpose of the company are pushed aside. This inescapably depresses the hopes of the real industrialist, and if he lasts for more than 18 months in his "new" position, then that is the exception rather than the rule. Most corporations on taking over an enterprise, however, prefer to sack the chief executive, in exchange for a golden handshake, before placing a financial Whiz-kid into his former position.

8 – How consumers lose out to the multiples

If that is a glance at the micro-economic effects of dispossession, then the macro-economic effects are even more dire. Democracy with any degree of integrity in society becomes impractical if a broad base of the population as *individuals* do not own and control the means of production, distribution, and the means of exchange. When business ownership bodies exceed a certain size, as they do with corporations, there comes a point when they dictate consumer choice, or create a situation (through monopoly) when choice is manipulated or removed. In the retailing of foodstuffs, for example, they often act as a barrier between producers and the intelligent consumer in the sense of offering aesthetically appealing products instead of better tasting, or healthier or otherwise superior quality products.

Whilst independents work in competition through diversity, through the presentation and choice of products they prefer to offer, corporations aim at a universal standard to suit all tastes, which results in blandness and the reduction of quality. They then resort to illusion and psychology in forcing their products on a gullible public through the myth and magic of costly advertising on TV, the press, and billboards. In this way both specific and generic products lose the essence of their reality through a brand name or association with a particular retail outlet. This is to be contrasted sharply with the open and diversified markets of independent outlets, always in a state of flux, always in direct personal contact with the customer, and always adapting to natural circumstances and change as the seasons, local variations, and differing needs.

A population deprived of business ownership is naturally at the mercy of influences over which it has no control in every sphere of commercial activity. Corporate power is concentrated power and will begin by destroying smaller units of competition until they are annihilated. But power is self-generating, and when great power has annihilated and accumulated all that it originally sought, it will then seek to diversify in further extending that power. This has been demonstrated clearly over the past decades with the expansion of retail markets, but often such diversity, whilst being financially successful, lacks the specialism and expertise in pursuing these new activities. The diversification of major supermarkets into selling financial services may be cited as such an example. Nonetheless, it is defended in the name of *free markets*, but such freedom would better serve consumer needs and be more trustworthy if pursued by professionals in the independent sector.

When separate corporations of various kinds unite for a common purpose, it is then they are most dangerous to the public interest. Such purposes are, of course, economic, but on such a scale they take on a political dimension. The huge might of corporations – especially those which are transnational – are so powerful and blatant in their ambition, that they have bought themselves into all parliamentary groups of any significance, and corrupted the political system to its core. The takeover of the political system by global capitalism has succeeded entirely in destroying representative democracy: firstly, through alienating party politics from the electorate in breaking the essential representative connection with the people; and secondly, through the fact that business and company law, and especially international business is unaccountable to any democratic authority, or any other authority external to its existence, apart only from the Inland Revenue and HM Customs and Excise, and that legislation concerned with Health and Safety, and the protection of employees' rights.

9 – How corporate power homogenises taste and annihilates individuality

But all the above powers together are of little relevance in confronting the overwhelming strength of the financial-industrial system as a political force. This is because through the formation of their own pressure groups, which may be founded to accomplish a huge raft of purposes for directly or indirectly serving their ends, they supplant the democratic elements of the legislature. Over the past 60 years, throughout the industrialised world, there has been an acceleration of financial power substituting that of the electorate through subtle and secret means.

This is often achieved through corporations adopting an avuncular or charitable attitude towards society, and so whilst on the one hand they advertise widely their philanthropic motives, on the other hand, they not only accumulate for themselves ten times or a hundred times the value of their alleged giving, but they push around and re-shape society as they will in enhancing their own profitability. An obvious example of the latter may be seen through the activities of property developers over the past 30 years, for whilst they have pushed up values to intolerable limits, they have at the same time constantly reduced the living space of domestic accommodation, so that people are now obliged to live in matchbox houses with all the discomfort and inconvenience which this entails.

All such concentrated financial power culminates in people losing their freedom and those values of individualism characterising the full development of personality, together with the full enjoyment of intellectual and spiritual potential, marking off one person from another. This is made evident through the exaggerated standardisation of thought, taste, and attitudes, imposed by advertising in satisfying corporate greed. In this way the majority are desensitised, and the homogenising of society in serving purely commercial interests, or those created for profit alone, separates the inclinations of the individual from the better part of his individuality. Hence life becomes cheapened and made ever more trivial, and concerned with transient feelings rather than more permanent values giving a purposeful dimension to life.

Carried to their extreme, these tendencies are most clearly manifested in all those characteristics we most despise in the unique American character – reflecting attitudes and motivations wholly and rightfully despised by the rest of humanity. It is then that superficiality and the repudiation of the idea of values as having any objective reality is set upon a pedestal. Is this to be the ultimate fate of civilisation? If so, it means the latter will turn in on itself towards a course of catastrophic decline and ultimate collapse.

CHAPTER 5
Contemporary problems no longer lend themselves to a class-based interpretation

"There is no better way of heading off the nightmare of unified political action by the economically disadvantaged that might issue in common demands than to set different groups of the disadvantaged against one another."

Brian Barry, *Culture and Equality*, Polity, 2001, pp. 11-12.

1 – A scientific approach and the relevance of democracy 2 – Democracy and its need for Creative Conflict 3 – The left/right divide was the Creative Conflict of the recent past 4 – Alienation of the majority from established politics 5 – Justice and equity achieved through the evolution of democracy 6 – The end of the road for the left/right divide 7 – How the old divide is now counter-productive 8 – The blindness of opinion-formers and politicians to this fact 9 – The transformation of the classes 10 – Individualism and the burdens of responsibility

1 – A scientific approach and the relevance of democracy

Having looked at the present condition of humanity in the advanced industrial world, we must now place this in its correct political context. In discussing the social environmental, or other problems of humanity, or that of any particular society, with the purpose of their resolution, it is futile to do so without attempting to place them within a clear political context. Such discussions may otherwise be engaging, controversial, profound, or in some other way illuminating, but they cannot hope to produce those answers which lead to effective action. We live in the real world and must act accordingly.

The expression of mere good intentions are useless, as also are utopian visions with no basis in material fact. Worst of all are those discussions on terrestrial problems which are allowed to merge into the religious-type dimension. This occurs when discussion becomes too heavily involved in general or abstract principles, usually entailing questions of right or wrong; when practicalities become disconnected from aims, and all hopes are made to lie in the outcome of a few nebulous ideas. Such situations have occurred too readily throughout history, and the causes originally giving rise to controversy are never satisfactorily examined. It is therefore our intention to approach these questions from a scientific aspect, and this means a sociological approach, usually through examining the evidence of history linked to economic and psychological factors.

Good government is what all peoples throughout our planet yearn for. In the industrialised world the majority insist that any such good government must be *democratic* government, but just as democratic government is not necessarily good, so likewise non-democratic government is not necessarily bad. Over the past 150 years several of the finest regimes, defined in terms of fulfilling the material and social interests of the majority, have been authoritarian, but none of these have emerged from the stable of populist or Marxist socialism. This may be disconcerting since it seems to cast a shadow over the universality of democratic aspirations of ordinary working people. Socialism has proved a disaster as a political system on two counts: firstly, because its failure to appreciate the psychological dynamic of the business process led to economic decline; and secondly, because mismanagement and incompetence have led in turn to famine, bloodshed and injustice on a scale unprecedented since the Mongol invasions or Biblical times.

Two of the most successful governing regimes over the past 150 years have been Bismarck's Germany in the 19th century, comprising social reforms imitated throughout the civilised world; and Lee Kuan Yew's rule in Singapore. Both these regimes entailed top-down authoritarianism, but their success was due to highly professional management, and the purpose and achievement of raising the educational standards of their peoples to a very high level. It may be noted that all Lee Kuan Yew's ministers held PhD degrees. In addition, both governmental regimes sought and succeeded in establishing socially peaceful societies, relatively free of those class conflicts which so divided and tore apart the peoples of more democratic countries. Authoritarianism, of course, is quite distinct from totalitarianism, for in the first, intellectual and artistic life may be allowed free development (as it was in the two regimes cited) whilst impediments may be placed on political activity. Totalitarianism, on the other hand, of both left and right, allows little if any freedom in regards to many aspects of life, dictates the parameters of intellectual and artistic life, and is generally oppressive.

Are we therefore disdaining the idea of democratic government as somehow ineffective? No, we shall argue that democratic government linked to the needs of a democratic society are both desirable and *essential* components for the eventual happiness and full development of all peoples, but that democracy has limitations with regard to its practical implementation, and this calls for candid recognition. In the previous chapter we remarked on the carelessness and irresponsibility of governments and their advisers in their approach to both the idea and establishment of democratic regimes on foundations of sand.

2 – Democracy and its need for Creative conflict

Democracy as a reality needs to be treated with greater respect. It is not something to be bestowed as the gesture of a patronising gift by the technologically advanced upon the naivety of undeveloped tribal peoples. Democracy, in the not too distant past, as we have noted above, has proved unworkable even amongst highly civilised cultures, and so how can it be expected to succeed amongst peoples with the simplest forms of political organisation? Democracy is even now supposedly established amongst old and respected civilisations, but the reality of its existence remains questionable in witnessing the poverty, injustice, and inequity amongst their helpless masses in these particular nation states. Democracy cannot simply be created through the brush of a magic wand, but rather through the often painful development of a long political tradition.

It is absurdly naïve to imagine that democracy can simply be established by setting in place a set of administrative arrangements, and announcing the formation of ready-made political parties. A democratic system must be integral to the culture, thought patterns, and traditions of a people. If it is not, there is little hope for that essential two-way connecting link between representatives and their electorates, without which democracy is meaningless. The representation of ideas and policies, and the longer term pursuit of their purpose, will not be understood, if democracy consists of formal institutions alone without the existence of a common understanding amongst the majority. Democracy demands the participation of people throughout every sector of society.

It should also be understood that democracy cannot exist without the presence of *creative* conflict. Such divisions need to express matters of *real* controversy and to reflect the existence of different groups with their own distinctive economic vested interests. Creative conflict means the organisation of these groups in such a way that they resolve their problems for the longer-term common good of all. That is the definition of the democratic process. It is an evolutionary process necessitating constant change at an indefinable rate, following the ongoing Hegelian dialectic of progress through thesis, antithesis, and synthesis.

Democracy calls for a slower rate of change than other systems of government, the latter tending to force change through sudden and violent upheavals. Democracy only comes into being during epochs of major crises, and is evoked through agreement amongst leading conflictual groups in society as a preferable mode for resolving differences as opposed to civil war or revolution. Such differences, therefore, tend to be intractable or complex in touching the profounder questions of government policy. They defy quick or sudden decision-making, and call for debate and gradualism which may last for generations.

Societal divisions giving rise to Creative conflict cannot merely be invented or assumed to exist in establishing democracy in a nation state. For example, what might conveniently be identified as tribal or language groups within a nation state, and then apportioning political parties to each, is unlikely to contribute to the making of sound democracy. It might not contribute to the intended purpose of *creative* conflict. This is because such differences would not only be irreconcilable from the start, but could have no basis in the formation of a democratic attitude. Such an approach would only succeed in arousing conflict where perhaps none had existed before. Creative conflict is only an option in sophisticated societies divided by complex or entangled economic interests. All these factors present extraordinary difficulties in establishing *representative* democracy in backward or developing territories, and helps explain why so many have foundered, usually degenerating into exploitative dictatorships ruled by tiny elites.

3 – The left/right divide was the Creative confict of the recent past

In the industrialised Western world, and wherever such an industrial pattern has followed in other territories, Creative conflict has taken the form of class conflict, or at least, this has been the path of history from the inception of the industrial revolution until approximately the 1960s. This, of course, has been marked by the conflict between capital and labour, or the proletariat versus the bourgeoisie, or Have-nots against Haves. To most, any other form of political conflict or political life still remains unimaginable. This is because the ideologies of parliamentary parties – or rather, the remnants of their ideologies, for we now supposedly live in a post-ideological age – are still based around the concept of the left/right divide.

All parties striving to be modern, in looking towards the future, would like to extricate themselves from this imprisoning stereotypical framework, but despite all their efforts, they are unable to do so. Whilst the Tories strive bravely to show their human face through their concern for the NHS, and the aged and poor; the Labour party meanwhile seeks to demonstrate its pro-business ethos for all the world to see. Whilst the Tories give rise to mistrust through their alternating hot and cold policies on lowering or raising taxation; Labour's pro-business policies amount to little more than promoting the usurious interests of large corporations, and in this they differ little from their opponents.

The reason for this dichotomy which is a mixture of hypocrisy and indecision, is that all the parties are riven by their own internal contradictions. To what extent should they or could be dominated by external financial-industrial interests? Despite all good intentions they are unable to maintain their integrity to themselves. The actuality today is that the political parties have become so lost through ditching ideology and resorting to the expediency of pragmatism, that they no longer know where they belong, and during election periods they put on such a false front that none except simpletons are prepared to accept their promises.

In looking towards the British General election in 2010, Andrew Rawnsley wrote that, "David Cameron can rely on first past the post to give him power on a low share of the vote. But a brittle mandate secured from a discredited voting system will not be a stable basis for a Conservative government which will have to take some wildly unpopular decisions. The Tories face having to implant spending cuts the like of which have not been seen in Britain for a quarter of a century. It is also highly likely that they will have to start their term in office putting up some taxes too. ... The decline of the big two is even more immediately frightening for Labour. During Labour's long period in the wilderness in the 1980s and 1990s, it was often conjectured that the party was doomed to permanent impotence and perhaps even extinction because of the shrivelling of the industrial working class who were the party's original base. When Labour lost four elections in a row, it became a regular topic of academic study and journalist commentary to ask can Labour ever win again?

"The question appeared to have been answered when along came Tony Blair to lead them to three consecutive election victories. His winning skills gave the impression that Labour's historic decline had been arrested, even reversed. Yet it now looks more likely that his three victories merely put a temporary mask on the deeper trend. New Labour's electoral strength was founded on his gifts as a communicator and adroit political positioning, the suicidal tendencies of the Tories during that period and a long economic boom fuelled by debt. Take away all those special factors and Labour's long-term decline becomes manifest again."[10]

When the leader of the Liberals, Nick Clegg, recently exclaimed, "the duopoly that dominated British politics in the 20th century is dying on its feet," he may have been right, but he should also be reminded "that people who live in glass houses shouldn't throw stones!" As I have argued elsewhere in this book, centrist third parties always tend to fall between two stools, whilst achieving little to break the age-old political mould. A far more perceptive MP is James Purnell, who resigned from the Cabinet in despair at Gordon Brown to lead a 3-year project for Demos in looking to collaborate with imaginative left-wingers, when he so rightly declared that, "we and the Tories are still flogging 20th century arguments."

4 – Alienation of the majority from established politics

The real situation is that political life in the industrialised world has reached a crisis point which is little understood. It amounts to not only a major crisis, but of a kind which has never occurred before in human history. Its cause and consequences must therefore be explained. There has emerged a total bifurcation between the 97 ½%+ majority of the population and their rulers, which has occurred through stealth over the past 60 years. The cause is the transformation of society and the world of work over that period, and the gradual (even unconscious) alienation which has developed between the population and the forces of financial power.

This alienation has been expressed through the many millions supporting single issue causes, usually environmental,

---

[10] Andrew Rawnsley, op. cit.

and the collapse of support for more conventional political groups. These single issue causes confirm the underlying concern of the majority with political issues, and offer channels for diverting a sense of frustration with our current situation, but they are a poor and quite unsatisfactory substitute for involvement in general or holistic politics in resolving the greater national and international issues of our age. It is therefore wrong and inaccurate for cynical opinion-formers to proclaim the public is politically apathetic on the grounds it has turned its back on the established political parties, when the real truth is that the public have resorted to one-sided or narrow causes, which only partially begin to represent their interests, as a last desperate hope for a better world. But such a second-best choice is, of course, better than none at all.

Although class struggle in England may be traced from the 1530s, following the sack of the monasteries, we are here only concerned with the industrial age from the second half of the 18th century, and we can say that from the mid-19th century onwards – in Britain from the time of the Chartist movement in the 1840s – class struggle became politically overt and clearly recognised by society, as the proletariat and bourgeoisie hardened their stance in safeguarding their separate interests. At first this was manifested through the Combinations, the early activities towards trades unionism, demonstrations and strikes, and only later through the work of political parties. But from the beginning there was a process of give and take, and the recognition that demands should be met halfway, and democracy alone became the instrument for resolving differences in much of Europe.

In those territories with more authoritarian regimes, there were periods of revolution followed by top-down initiatives legislating for better conditions and wages and even rights – at least in Western Europe. By the 20th century democratic government became the norm in ensuring equity and justice throughout society, although in those socialist countries where capitalism was overthrown entirely, democracy took on a different meaning, viz., the "dictatorship of the proletariat," which in reality meant the replacement of democracy with political oppression.

5 – Justice and equity achieved through the evolution of democracy

The recognition of the left/right did not emerge from the ideas of opposing ideologies, it arose inevitably from the *factual* recognition amongst all sectors of society and political groups of the divide between Haves and Have-nots. The right formed their own attitudes and policies in resolving difficult social issues, from the charitable and philanthropic style of legislation initiated through the work of the 7th Earl of Shaftesbury, to the personal schemes of the Prince Consort, who so irritated several of the leading statesmen of his time, to the important social legislation of Disraeli during his second administration between 1874-1880, to the State Socialism of Bismarck throughout the 1880s, which sought to deflate the largest socialist movement in Europe through extensive reforms and pension and insurance arrangements of a kind which had never been seen before.

The rich and powerful, of course, never desired the existence of class struggle or the left/right divide, and although they may correctly be viewed as the former oppressors of the working class, they must nonetheless be given appropriate credit for their practical initiatives in creating a more just and egalitarian society.

As I have argued elsewhere, the left have always exaggerated, through myth and propaganda, the role of the working class or trades unionism in raising the material living standards of their members. Socialism was itself the invention of highly educated men from privileged backgrounds, whilst the ordinary working man was so helpless and ill-informed that he could not have begun to think through the practical implications needed in changing society. His only ability was to cry in pain or resort to violence. The truth, therefore, is that the parties of the right deserve almost equal credit in lifting the masses from their misery as those of the left. In Britain, the fact that the

Tories held office for a significantly longer period than Labour in the 20th century up to the year 1979, stands as evidence for this. The Tory party always had a strong reformist element amongst its leadership until that latter date.

The ideas of American management gurus from early in the 20th century onwards in alleviating the discontent of workers through psychological means alone, e.g., Taylorism, which may have crept into legislation in the States, and much later in Europe, cannot of course, be credited as contributing to genuine reform or justice in improving the lot of the oppressed since, as with so many things American, it was based on trickery and deceit. American initiatives towards a more socially just or egalitarian society have usually been flawed, primarily because of their political establishment's ideological conviction that the first – if not the only – purpose of business is to maximise stockholders' returns far exceeds that of any to be found in any part of Europe.

The outcome of the evolution of democracy in the non-American world, is that mainstream parliamentary parties of the right (as well as obviously those of the left) of all advanced industrial economies in both the East and West, not only accept the following in principles but seek to implement them in practice:-

1. That equality of opportunity should be available to all;
2. That democratic government should be advanced as the best medium in promoting the will and welfare of the people;
3. That school education should be free and compulsory, and that a university education should be made financially available to all those of sufficient ability, irrespective of background;
4. That health arrangements, free at the point of need, should be made available for all nationals either directly funded by the State, or by competing national insurance institutions under the dirigiste authority of the State;

5. That old age pension arrangements preferably equivalent to two thirds of last leaving salary should be made available to all;

6. That effective safety nets should be put in place to assist the unemployed, the insolvent, the mentally impaired, and others who are no longer able to care for themselves for whatever reason; and,

7. That all nationals should be regarded and treated as equal irrespective of race, religion, other beliefs, sexual orientation, or social origin.

6 – The end of the road for the left/right divide

As I have argued at length in another book, not only is America no longer a democracy, primarily because plutocratic forces have penetrated and then neutered democratic mechanisms, but she is ideologically opposed to state intervention in the social field which protects the individual, on the grounds that it is "socialist," "dictatorial," and an "unwarranted tax burden" on the people. The outcome of these attitudes has led inevitably to widespread inhumanity as reflected through a popular hardened view towards all categories of unfortunates. This is reflected through poverty, soaring crimes rates, and by far the largest per capita prison population to be found anywhere in the world.

With regard to the better half of the industrialised world throughout the Euro-Asian landmass and further afield, the above seven points and their political significance pose an interesting situation. What remains of the substantive differences between the right and left? Of course there is ongoing debate as to how the above reforms may be implemented or furthered, and as to their time-scale and financial viability, but beneath this, there nonetheless remains the genuine moral commitment to eventually see these through. The evils of Thatcherism have hopefully been ditched forever and a repetition of the callous pronouncements of Tory leaders in the 1980s would be inconceivable today – although in fairness it should be noted they were made in response to the provocation of equally malign tactics of extremists on the left.

The left and right still, of course, retain a distant and hazy view of their ideological origins, which supposedly, and in theory, directs their thinking and the formulation of policy. But as we demonstrate below, external and unanticipated forces, have cut the ground beneath the ideological foundations of all established parliamentary groups There is a feeling of deep unease in political life today. There remains only a partial realisation amongst politicians that not only is there *in fact* a lack of real difference between the left and right in regard to ultimate aims, but more seriously, there is no reason why such difference *should* exist.

Therefore, politicians are reduced to scraping the bottom of the barrel for any muck to throw at their opponents, and this rather than gaining votes, only brings them into greater disdain with the public. But what can they do? They remain chained to the bankrupt remnants of their ideological origins, and it is this which prevents an intelligently constructive approach. It is the need for *new thinking* which defines the political crisis of our time, but new thinking is impossible until the existing political mould is shattered. Only then can a new vision be created. At this point it would be useful to look at those external factors which have cut the ground from beneath our politicians' feet.

7 – How the old divide is now counter-productive

As we remarked at the start of this book, over the past 200 years the evolutionary democratic process has now completed its task in resolving socio-economic issues through the medium of the left/right divide – and completed it successfully. It should be understood we are *not* stating that all socio-economic issues have been resolved, but only that they have been resolved as far as the particular *medium* of the left/right divide can settle such questions.

The outcome of this is that our political parties have been left stranded – high and dry – in a kind of no-man's land, where they are separated from their former electoral supporters by a wide margin of rough and foamy sea, with dangerous undercurrents and uncertain winds. Our politicians would therefore risk their very existence by attempting to swim across such a threatening strait in re-joining those who would cast them a friendly vote.

This medium of Creative conflict has successfully completed its task through socio-economic legislation in equalising the chances of all for maximising their opportunities in life in so far as the democratic medium of the left/right divide can carry them. That is, a point has been reached through the use of this democratic method whereby further political activity expressed through the medium becomes counter-productive to the public good. Until approximately the 1960s, the ding-dong or class-based confrontational politics, was still constructive in advancing the cause of social progress.

This is because society at that time was still clearly marked by a distinctive proletariat with its own socio-economic and cultural interests which were separate from those of the middle and upper classes. All were aware of these factors at the time, and the left/right divide continued to resolve its differences through a wide variety of measures. Whilst many of those from a privileged background with a strong social conscience sought to promote change either through parties of the left or right; those from the working classes meanwhile strove and succeeded in improving their material lot, and consequently rose in their own estimation of themselves and in the eyes of those around them. These new changes and attitudes not only eroded proletarianism, but also the outlook and status of the bourgeoisie.

Old class-based values withered everywhere, and new attitudes and new conditions of life gave rise to new values – or the potential for such values. A middle-middle majority emerged, but was so heterogeneous in its external characteristics as at first not to be recognisable even as a new class. The only true criterion for its existence as a class – or for the existence of any class – were the unique economic circumstances in which it found itself. The counter-productive effects of politics driven through the medium of the left/right divide, irrespective of whether the appeal to class divisiveness is explicit (as with the far left) or cleverly hidden as with the majority of parliamentary groups at the present time, is manifested through the following:-

1. The lack of credibility, or seeming exaggeration, or distortion of factual reality of politicians when they press their arguments, especially in confrontational situations with the opposition;

2. The deceit which this conveys to the public, who in their better judgement, choose to walk away from the established parties;

3. The recognition that the discussion and resolution of issues are obfuscated and hindered when subjected to the viewpoints of the left/right divide;

4. The recognition that the major problems of the 21st century (e.g., environmental issues) cannot properly be discussed through resorting to ding-dong politics without constructing a complex and unreal ideological framework;

5. The realisation by the middle-middle majority, that as the addressees of their established politicians, they no longer fit the stereotypes of being seen as proletarians or as a bourgeoisie, and hence the messages directed to them are met by deaf ears; and,

6. That the political exploitation of the left/right divide, howsoever transmitted, is morally indefensible in that it is inescapably based on external cultural differences and appearances, for which the individual cannot be responsible any more than the Afro-Caribbean can be held responsible for the colour of his skin.

8 – The blindness of opinion-formers and politicians to this fact

It should be understood that the evolutionary democratic process far transcends political parties or their ideologies, and that the former may crush the latter through the unstoppable juggernaut of history. Our politicians of earlier generations may have succeeded in achieving a wonderful task – but only as unconscious agents – and they could not possibly anticipate the outcome of their work. They worked merely as cogs within a huge machine of which they had little inkling. It is almost a certainty that if those politicians and ideologues of the past, of both left or right, could rise from their graves and witness the eventual outcome of their lives' mission, they would cry in bewilderment, "but we never intended to design such a society!" However advanced or good such a society might be, these minions from the past would be incapable of understanding or appraising its qualities or values.

This is not only because the future is always unknown, and never materialises as might be imagined, but because we are all prisoners of the present, and even when we glorify our vision of the future, the latter is never actualised according to exact predictions. That is, our idea of the future is always limited by our imprisonment within the present. All this helps explain the blindness of politicians and opinion-formers at the present time in failing to comprehend our contemporary condition, or their failure to imagine even an alternative to the vicious and intellectually destructive left/right divide as it currently exists. As the future inevitably defies what we can imagine, we must therefore be prepared, if necessary, to repudiate everything in the present if there may exist a better future the nature of which we cannot properly comprehend.

Even the practical erosion of left/right confrontational politics, the evidence of which is everywhere around us, still fails to convince our thinkers or academia that there might be other positive possibilities for the morrow. They cannot escape from all the false illusions, deceptive statistics, and jargon, and the piled-up useless knowledge which is about to collapse around their ears like a pack of cards. It would be helpful, therefore, to look at our actual situation as it exists today.

9 – The transformation of the classes

The situation needs to be approached from two perspectives: firstly, from that of a sociological description of the new majority; and secondly, from that of the transformation of the economic framework acting as a catalyst in creating an entirely new class, with political attitudes and aspirations quite different from any previous generation.

As we have noted, the heterogeneous middle-middle majority at the present time does not outwardly present any of the characteristics of a new class, except in a purely negative sense in repudiating the past. Those who have risen from the cloth-capped proletariat, may or may not regard themselves as "working class," and their opinions may veer from the far left to the BNP or Conservative right, but in any event their situation is such that the world outlook (*Weltanschauung*) of their parents or grandparents is quite unsuited to their present condition; or in promoting their better interests. Their historical origins may present the *vestiges* of a working class, and political ideology may attract them to this idea, but in reality they have been transformed into something different.

This change has not merely occurred through consumerism or better material standards (which in themselves mean little in sociological terms), but rather through education and responsibilities which have forced them out from the pattern of an earlier collectivism into an individualistic mould. This individualism has not emerged as a matter of choice or lifestyle, but out of necessity in meeting the accelerating demands in the division of labour, whereby aptitude and inclination decide the occupation of a man or woman, and not the traditional influences of parents or close relations. This diversity, which calls upon each individual to maximise his or her personal interests with regard to earnings linked to aptitude, and the raft of responsibilities following on from the greater complexity of life, necessitates a total change away from the proletarian perspective of life.

The conditions of contemporary life, therefore, contrast sharply with those of proletarian conditions existing 60 or more years ago. The old proletariat were easily pushed around, and provided it was by members of their own class they hardly resented it. The trades unions and Workings men's clubs, and other working class associations, were hemmed around with all kinds of intrusive rules and regulations, intolerable to the middle class mentality. They were usually concerned with regulations on matters that the higher echelons of society took for granted – and hence they were an impudence if expressed in black and white. Proletarian life was narrow and conformist, rarely concerned with anything beyond its own immediate material needs. As workers were huddled together in the great factories, mines, or shipyards of the past, so in their leisure hours they enjoyed the organising collectivism of the holiday camp or the bright lights and switchbacks of Blackpool.

Those amongst their number who were "thinking people" joined the Labour party, but not in a spirit of enquiry for objective knowledge, but in resentment and hatred in engaging in the great game of class warfare. They sought to develop their conspiratorial abilities through trades union activity, with the distant dream of bringing down the "establishment." As their aims were revolutionary – albeit slow-motion revolution of the English kind – and their methods negative, i.e., striking, marching, or fighting in the streets, there was little chance of anything creative emerging directly from their efforts. What good that did emerge was *indirect*, i.e. the response of decision-making and legislation imposed from above in alleviating social ills. Nonetheless, the left sought to take credit for all such reforms, but they could only do this through creating the myth of the heroic working class, and this was supported by the carrying of religious-type banners, activities more associated with the Orthodox or Catholic churches than the world of politics.

10 – Individualism and the burdens of responsibility

Such attitudes and activities amongst the new middle-middle majority would be inconceivable in our own time. The children and grandchildren of such proletarians of a former era are too busy and burdened by so many personal responsibilities, differing from one individual to another, that they would neither have the inclination nor opportunity for such collectivism. For example, further education or training has now become a lifelong recurring experience for most people, whilst the education of children is all-important, and together with extra-curricular activities, calls for the constant guidance and monitoring by parents in a way it did not before. Meanwhile, house ownership is accompanied by the innumerable responsibilities of maintenance, and the planning and budgeting that goes along with this.

Slums are only the product of public or Council housing, when the proletarian had little care or thought for the conditions in which he lived until rainwater dripped through his ceiling, or wet rot through rising damp caused his floorboards to collapse, in which event, with curses and threats, he would harass Council officials and leave the rest to them. But as soon as housing is privatised former slums are soon transformed into neat well-maintained areas, for there is nothing which succeeds in raising living standards so much as the responsibility entailed in personal ownership.

Other areas of responsibility entail the completion of complex tax declarations, and the necessity of attending to tax avoidance (usually in conjunction with accountants); the buying and selling of stocks and shares (now engaged in by many from working class backgrounds); forward planning with regard to earnings in preparation for retirement and the possible burdens of old age; and most significantly, the greater division of labour and explosion in the number of smaller business units (although not of ownership as we have noted above), and consequently, all the responsibilities of business management. All these individual responsibilities are necessarily character changing towards a more personal and confidential style of life, and with certainty they undermine every aspect of proletarian collectivism.

The remnants of the old working class, which of course include many amongst the new middle-middle majority, often bemoan the passing of a former era with its comforting solidarity. They complain, and rightly, that society has become too selfish and self-centred – even atomised, and that many natural social bonds which united people in the past have been lost forever. But these fears need not be nurtured. Humankind was always social at its core and will remain so. At the present time in the advanced industrialised world society is undergoing a kind of interregnum.

There is a suspension in the relationship between the highly heterogeneous middle-middle majority and its consciousness as a community, with regard to its connectedness with the State or ruling authority. If there was any truth in Margaret Thatcher's contention that society does not exist but only the individuals of which it is composed, it can only be understood in the sense of this abnormal or temporarily suspended state of alienation. Such a situation *is* only temporary – and such interregnums have occurred before. Society today in the advanced industrial world is fraught with uncertainty and apprehension about the future, and even listless in the face of hype and falsity it is daily fed by the media and government agencies.

Amongst those of goodwill there exists a spirit of toleration of cultural difference, whilst the intolerance which political parties would stir amongst themselves and then amongst the population have become intolerable to all. Hence there is no leadership or inspiring ideas to extricate humankind from its precarious condition to point towards a better future. But the catalyst for a better future will not be brought about by the parliamentary pandemonium of our petty politicians, but rather by the transformation of the economic framework dictating the destiny of us all. And here we come to consider that second perspective, referred to above, which will transform the middle-middle majority into the reality of a new political class.

CHAPTER 6
The political parties have sold out to usurious financial interests

"If it be so, shame, scandal, and contempt
attend their covetous thoughts; need make their
graves!
Usurer they live, and may they die like slaves."

Thomas Heywood, *A Woman Killed With Kindness*,
(1603) Act IV, Sc. II.

1 – The irrationalism and harm of financial markets   2 – Reconstruction and not reform is called for   3 – The ills of Rentier and global capitalism   4 – Why the left refrain from challenging globalisation   5 – Today's major issues do not lend themselves to knockabout politics   6 – Whilst Rentier economies destroy the environment, Productive economies work for its rescue   7 – Why today's economic issues are no longer class-based   8 – Why the new majority disdain class-based politics   9 – The Universal economic issues of our time   10 – These issues are dismissed by the left as representing middle class "interests"   11 – The left is blind to injustice against the new majority

1 – The irrationalism and harm of financial markets

Although the proponents of globalisation may play down its existence by suggesting it is little more than the next logical step in the evolution of international trade, in reality it is much more than that, for in different ways it adversely impacts on the lives of peoples throughout the world irrespective of the stage of their industrial development.

The most significant fact factor about globalisation is not the international sale and exchange of tangible goods, despite the unprecedented enlargement of such trade, but rather the purely speculative activity of money creation or usury, through the profits to be made through the non-productive casino economy.

The daily risk-taking of astronomical amounts of financial capital has been exacerbated through the speed of its movement, enabled through contemporary and ever-changing information technology. The work of brokers in their need for speed of reaction has become essentially a high-testosterone activity, where cool judgement becomes problematical if not often impossible, and where rational decision-making is pushed aside through the fluctuating influence of markets towards any unanticipated direction.

But worse than this is the fact that the *outcome* of the work of financial professionals is beyond their own control or will. The purpose and *will* of brokers and others is the maximisation of money profits for investors, but in the speculative scrum of markets for greater share, the outcome is not only unpredictable but irrational. The factors influencing as to where capital will be driven around the globe, or as to the rise and fall of shares, are multifarious and unanticipated, whilst the predictions of financial advisers are little more scientific than the work of astrologers. Hence the day-to-day work of the highest earning professions on our planet produces results which are beyond their own control – or beyond the direct intentions and control of any other human agency.

Pure financial activity has created a monster with no knowing what benefits or destruction it is liable to inflict at any time in any part of the world. This is most clearly demonstrated through market crashes and recessions, or the collapse of banks, other financial institutions, or corporations engaged in any sphere of productivity. But less known, or publicised, are the impediments against promoting essential public works or projects, or the alleviation of social ills and poverty which is always present. Most obvious in these spheres is the need to confront global warming and diverse forms of environmental catastrophe, but because these crises fail to lend themselves to the demands of the usurious economy, they are constantly pushed aside as matters for "tomorrow" – that is, if their existence as problems are not denied in the first place.

2 – Reconstruction and not reform is called for

Criminality within the financial services industry is everywhere apparent on a minor scale, and often apparent on a major scale as witnessed through recent prosecutions and convictions; but it can never be over-emphasised that criminality (as legally defined) within the profession, is an evil of minor proportions by comparison with the systemic evils in the usury of Rentier capitalism. Hence all attempts to clean up the financial services industry, whether through self- or external regulation are doomed to failure. The evil lies not in greed or bad intentions – the naïve and usual accusation of religiously motivated simpletons, for these are natural and irremovable qualities inherent in the imperfection of all humankind – but rather in the irrationality of bad financial systems that cannot but corrupt even those of the greatest probity.

Over the past three decades, through the invention of ever-more ingenious money-making products, or the incorporation of newly designed usurious mechanisms – most emanating from America before extending their tentacles globally – there has developed in a non-legal sense, a criminal network of financial services, all of them constructed through the skill and foresight of America's huge army of professional lawyers. The term *criminal* in this context is justified, firstly through the deceit and ulterior motives of many such services; and secondly, and more significantly, through the destruction of manufacturing, the uprooting of self-sustainable communities, the impoverishment of millions, and the misery caused to many in every sector of society in every country on earth.

The answer to the above social problems in correcting the abuses of our financial-industrial system, is not to attempt tinkering reforms with existing institutions (for these lead nowhere and are usually evaded), being the approach of established parties across the political spectrum; and neither is it attempts to make men and women more virtuous, which is the hope of the left-leaning intelligentsia, judging from the feeble response of their journalistic contributions to every scandal which arises. The answer can only be found through the total overhaul of existing institutions, or their reconstruction from a strictly teleological perspective. Their social good can only be judged from the final outcome of their activities, and such an outcome can only be assured through their careful design and control at every level of their operation.

Results must no longer be left to trusting in an "invisible Hand." Such institutions must be established as rational organisations, and their staff at all levels must be channelled by regulations holding them to account for the socially beneficial outcome of their efforts. How this may be achieved is described in later chapters. Energetic, acquisitively-motivated and high-testosterone people may indeed be employed, but the framework within which they operate rather than their own margin of discretion, should guarantee they contribute to the cause of Productive Profitability as opposed to usurious accumulation.

James Buchan has argued that, "any new financial order for the world must tackle three chief challenges of our age. The first is the privileges enjoyed by people in the banking and securities trade on a scale which would not have shamed the nobility of the *ancien régime*. The second is the perverse character of modern investment by which financial surpluses generated by hard-working countries are channelled by the banks not to undeveloped nations that might turn them into prosperous future markets, but to the spoiled and elderly economies of Western Europe and the United States, already awash with unproductive capital. The third is our most pressing engagement, which is to prevent further ravages to the natural environment and the general amenity of existence from the reckless combination of the previous two challenges."[11]

Further on in the article, he continues, "at the heart of banking is a suicidal strategy. Banks take money from the public or each other on call, skim it for their own reward and then lock the rest up in volatile, insecure and illiquid loans that at times they cannot redeem without public aid. Put another way, the assets of the banking system belong to the joint-stock banks, but their liabilities (as we have learned in the past two months) are always and only public liabilities. ... So what is to be done with the banks? My own modest proposal ... is to take away from joint-stock banks the privilege of limited liability which they

---

[11] James Buchan, "The Fire Next Time," *New Statesman*, 17th November 2008.

abuse every moment of the day. … More realistically, now is the time for government authorities to begin slowly to peel back some of the other privileges, such as deposit insurance, that under the guise of protecting the public, merely protects the banker."

3 – The ills of Rentier and global capitalism

The ills of globalisation may be said to have already been established in the Anglo-Saxon countries and most Third world territories by the 1980s, especially as promoted by Reagan-Thatcherite economic policies, but it was not until the 1990s that American financial practices penetrated Continental Europe and the Far East Tigers to a significant degree, and began undermining their production bases with catastrophic results.

The ills of Rentier capitalism, being the technical term in defining and describing the economic mechanisms of globalisation have been analysed in my book, *Social Capitalism in Theory and Practice*, and this work should be consulted for a proper study of the subject. The arguments presented will not be repeated here, but the following summary is necessary before continuing the theme of this book:-

1. Globalisation politically disempowers peoples worldwide through the substitution of governmental power by financial-industrial forces, primarily through international agencies, off-shore tax havens, etc., which go over the heads of national authorities.
2. Globalisation is economically disadvantageous to the middle-middle majorities of the advanced industrial economies, as well as to the majorities of all other nation states.
3. It is disadvantageous to middle-middle majorities through the accumulation of capital into ever fewer hands, and the consequent process of universal dispossession in both the domestic and business spheres of activity.

4. Dispossession in the domestic sphere is effected through the inflation of property values, and the eventual reduction of property owners to tenants paying extortionate rents.

5. Dispossession in the business sector is effected through the speculative accumulation of enterprises by groups and corporations for the purpose of maximising investors' returns, and this in turn transforms the rationale and *modus operandi* of business thereby undermining its productivity and service to the consumer.

6. Globalisation is disadvantageous to majorities throughout the Third world in that –
   a) Slave labour conditions are created in manufacturing enterprises, whereby none of the lessons or benefits fought for and achieved in the advanced industrial economies may be freely passed on to the downtrodden and uninformed.
   b) Cash crops entail the dispossession of peasants from their land by giant corporations, and the dispossessed lose their self-sustainable status as they are herded into slums in mega-cities.

7. Globalisation is openly critical of and politically opposes any form of state-sponsored social welfare, irrespective of whether it is concerned with free health services, unemployment or sickness benefits, student grants for further education, or old age pensions, on the *given* grounds that welfare is "Socialistic" and hence an unwarranted tax burden on the people, but on the *real* grounds that such services fail to reward investors or contribute to the cause of usury as the first priority of economic activity.

8. Globalisation hinders public works, or state-sponsored emergency appeals (as we saw in 2005 when hurricane Katrina devastated New Orleans, flooding 80% of the city), or projects in protecting the environment or countering the ills of global warming, through oppressive interest rate arrangements restricting the raising of capital in exacerbating public debt.

5 – Why the left refrain from challenging globalisation

In view of the above, it may therefore seem astonishing that no parliamentary group in any advanced industrial state has effectively attempted to question – let alone oppose – the advance of globalisation. It might have been anticipated that the parties of the left would at some point have raised a small gesture of protest, but dumb silence has been their only non-response. There are several reason for this, and these may be enumerated as under:-

1. That globalisation is too large and powerful a force to be questioned – and certainly to be challenged – and hence it should be accepted passively as a *fait accompli.*
2. That it is promoted, both ideologically as well as in practice, by the USA, and as that country is the mightiest in the world, on those grounds it would be inexpedient to offer a challenge.
3. That the financial and economic manifestations of globalisation are too complex to disentangle, and because of this, it is best to go along with the tide.
4. The political left as well as the political right have always been attracted by gigantism in the industrial sphere, and hence the left are intuitively not too concerned by the ubiquitous threat of globalisation, even though it may conflict with their original political principles.

The above points clearly demonstrate both the incapacity and feebleness of the left in challenging the greatest political issue of our time. It further underlines their ignorance and unwillingness to consider even or attempt to understand the nature of financial-industrial issues. Not merely back bench MPs but even leading statesmen of the left blithely dismiss such questions as "above their heads." Such an attitude, in view of its implications, is truly preposterous! The fact that a situation cannot be challenged because it is too "big" or "powerful" turns our politicians into "surrender monkeys"

Evil is not obliterated through appeasement but rather made all the greater. History has no greater lesson than this. But the real problem of the left in confronting the question of globalisation is not cowardice or ignorance, but a lack of intellectual imagination in analysing our condition, and then designing an appropriate strategy in defeating the evil. But before turning to these questions, we must first describe the catalyst in transforming the middle-middle majority into a new political class in preparation for overturning political life as we know it.

5 – Today's major issues do not lend themselves to knockabout politics

The major problems facing society today throughout the advanced industrial world have ceased to be class-based. This is either because they are *universal* economic problems affecting those across the broad spectrum of society, or because they are *planetary* problems transcending the mere existence of the human species. Whilst the universal problems are concerned with issues of human justice, planetary problems are concerned with the survival of life in all its forms.

Democratic systems throughout the world today are totally unfitted to address either of these two sets of problems, both of which threaten catastrophe. Of the two, perhaps planetary issues should be given the higher priority since this may entail the eventual extinction of all fauna and flora, but the irony is that mainline political awareness (because of traditional thinking) puts this in a secondary position to the universal issues. In any event, in today's world both sets of problems are subordinated to involvement with surface or superficial issues with *daily visibility*, which easily lend themselves to the knockabout politics of the left/right divide. The class-based division of society is the life-blood of our political system, without which democracy as we know it could not survive. Hence our politicians are locked into a futile pattern of conflict achieving little for the progress of humankind.

The great middle-middle majority, who are alienated from the political establishment, think differently from their masters.

In their enlightenment and grasp of contemporary reality they have moved ahead. As they have retreated in disgust from the parties of both the left and right, in their millions they have flocked to well-publicised single issue movements concerned with the environment and the preservation of life in its many forms. These bodies which may be well-financed by millions of individuals in isolation, and patronised by royalty and those prominent in academia, the arts, and sciences, are nonetheless limited in their field of activity.

They are high-profile but not powerful organisations, and in that lies their tragedy. They can demonstrate, and petition, and use their funds on the media in extending their memberships, but finally they are no more than lobbying organisations. In the end they stand as no more than suppliants before our duplicitous politicians. The latter, of course, will receive them with unctuous marks of respect, but despite a polite interchange, it is doubtful if much is positively achieved. Our unscrupulous politicians, irrespective of party, are entirely in the hands of powerful financial bodies – the majority having declared interests in corporate organisations which tie their hands entirely. In addition to that, as we have all learned over the past few years, a large proportion feed off the bribes of undeclared business interests.

The outcome of such a situation is that the middle-middle majority, who have transformed their political loyalties from the mainstream parties to single issue movements, remain politically impotent. They have chosen where to place their political loyalties and annual subscriptions, but single issue movements, irrespective of their numbers and financial backing, are no more than protest associations. The middle-middle majority are therefore faced with the necessity of somehow getting back into mainstream politics.

6 – Whilst Rentier economies destroy the environment, Productive economies work for its rescue

Parliamentary politicians, meanwhile, have ingenious ways of engaging positively in discussions on environmental issues, whilst at the same time evading successfully to achieve an effective outcome. The political reasons for this are not difficult to identify. The forces of global or Rentier capitalism have always been tardy, if not totally opposed to moves calling for serious measures to counter the threats of environmental catastrophe – and they still are. Until the recent past the American government dismissed allegations of climate change as the absurd invention of the left-wing intelligentsia. They employed their own scientists to demonstrate convincingly that the truth behind such allegations were due to "sun spot flares," or cyclical climate change, or merely freak weather conditions, but *not* due to man-made causes.

Such denials emanated from the per capita most polluting nation on earth, with powerful vested interests in maintaining the oil industry in its present filthy and obsolescent form, and other rust-bucket industries. Contrary to the received impression throughout most of the world, run-of-the-mill manufacturing industry in most of America is tumbledown and decrepit. German and English business friends who have visited the USA were astonished and then appalled at what they encountered. The explanation is to be found in the economic system of Rentier capitalism which withholds investment in new machinery or methods, etc., so that dividends may be maximised for stockholders. The inevitable consequence is that industry is only allowed to survive on the narrowest margins of existence. Only recently have the American authorities admitted that "perhaps" man-made climate warming might contribute to the melting of the polar ice-caps and the violence of seasonal hurricanes hitting her own continent.

All this may be contrasted with the situation in Continental Europe – particularly in the north. Throughout northern Continental Europe *real* steps have been achieved in meeting the challenge of climate warming and rising sea levels. Not only do ordinary people admit the existence of environmental issues, but their governments have invested huge amounts of capital in a wide variety of projects. Everywhere in Germany, Denmark, the Benelux countries, and further afield, there are electricity generating windtowers. In the same countries there are everywhere modern computer automated manufacturing plants housed in well-constructed factory buildings. Why is this? It cannot simply be dismissed as due to "cultural differences" or attitudes.

The reason is to be found in the tradition of a different economic system, viz., Productive capitalism primarily deriving its funds from the loans of credit investment industrial banks and not from equities managed by casino-like stock exchanges as in London or New York. As we have said in Chapter 4, this better economic system is now being undermined by American financial imperialism on a world scale, but Continental governments are still more protective towards their industries than in Britain or America.

If we turn to the situation in Britain, it is clearly evident we exist on the edge of an abyss on several fronts. Of all European countries we appear near the bottom with regard to investment in saving the environment. Whilst the media toy around with the comforting idea that man-made global warming is a "figment of the imagination," County Council authorities and amenity groups howl in protest against the construction of windtowers in ruining their vision of the countryside from their bedroom windows, in much the same way that protests were raised against the building of the railways 150 years ago.

Meanwhile, our Janus-faced politicians acknowledge the protests of the middle-middle majority, then fully accept the implications of global warming, and then go on to fudge every piece of legislation intended to reverse the problems confronting us. In Europe, whether it be in the parliament in Brussels or Strasbourg, or at one of the summits called from time to time, it is always British statesmen- or women who exasperate their colleagues from every other country with demands to "tone down" urgent legislation, or to introduce compromising clauses which nullify the effectiveness of what is required. Why is this? The given reason, or that which is intuitively understood by most, is that British people are moderate – perhaps over-cautious in their attitudes – and so seldom prepared to endorse legislation which is seemingly "sudden" or "too out of the ordinary." Such explanations, of course, are far from the real truth.

Nearer home, however, far worse situations threaten, and indeed, have actually occurred in the recent past. Britain's limited landmass has already been exposed to the ravages of climate warming, through flooding in low-lying areas and the erosion of our coastline. In the interior of our country dykes have broken, and thousands of properties – many of them new estates, have been flooded and rendered uninhabitable for months on end, with all the misery and costs this brings to house owners and their families. In other areas, huge swathes of farmland have been reduced to lakeland, ruining crops and drowning valuable livestock. County Councils, the National Farmers' Union, landowning associations, and other bodies, have approached central government for funding in re-building levees and coastal defences, but the response is always the same: the funds are not available!

The NFU have reiterated the economic argument that agricultural land needed to feed an increasing population is being lost forever, but even such an appeal falls on deaf ears. The response of government to such crises, in a country supposedly amongst the most cash-rich in the world, needs to be compared with the huge investments of a small country like the Netherlands in building polders, dykes, and other drainage and reclamation products. Furthermore, whilst over the past half century the Netherlands has been pro-active in increasing its total land area, Britain has merely been reactive or defensive in feeble attempts to minimise her land loss. What is the reason for this? Again, it stems from the Rentier capitalistic nature of our economic system, in contrast to the Netherlands which for over

400 years has been one of the most Productive capitalistic nations on earth.

The City of London, as always, has held back productivity and investment for all good purposes and for anything which protects the homeland. This is because its internal mechanism, as well as its interests, are internationally oriented, as also it is usurious. And because of the City's intrinsic characteristics, it could not attempt to operate otherwise. British governments of whatever hue, always have sufficient capital to finance American-driven wars, as the lap-dogs of that country, but seldom enough to relieve the misery of our own flood victims, or to compensate our farmers struggling to feed a growing population, or for that matter, to promote the prosperity of home-based industry.

7 – Why today's economic issues are no longer class-based

Although what we have cited as planetary problems must necessarily call on our first priority, it is the *universal* economic problems which are more likely to act as a catalyst in transforming the middle-middle majority into a new political class. This is because of the immediacy of the latter as issues of injustice, incompetence, or stupidity of government in overseeing the allocation of resources in enabling the full potential of people, or the alleviation of need. As such issues are concerned with justice and equity, it might be suggested they offer a suitable role for left-wing political activity, but as we explain below, this is far from the case.

This is primarily because these questions of need and equality of opportunity are not those of an underclass, but of *all*, across the entire spectrum of society. Hence there is no room here, or opportunity for identifying an enemy class to be confronted and knocked to the floor. The enemy is an impersonal economic system, vast in size and ubiquitous in its influence, but managed by an army of faceless brokers, bankers, financiers and clerks, who themselves are victims of the system, and hail from every sector of the community. By no definition do they constitute a class by comparison with anything that has existed previously. There is no opportunity here for the kind of resentment or hatred for flesh and blood beings in top hats or pin-striped suits which gave such satisfaction to the proletariat of an earlier period.

Of course myopic or corrupt politicians, or greedy property developers building matchbox houses, or ruthless loan sharks, or particular financiers, or the speculative directors of conglomerates may be attacked, but not as the collectivity of a class, but purely on the grounds of their mode of money-making, i.e., usury or productive wealth destroying economic activity. Money-making for personal gain is good if its *modus operandi* is Social Wealth Creation, and those who accumulate wealth according to such ethical standards deserve the full enjoyment of their well-gotten gains.

The others engaging in immoral activity may be identified easily through examining their business methods, but not as a distinctive class for three reasons:-

1. Because they are too heterogeneous to be projected as a class;

2. Because a class can only be properly defined in sociological terms through the characteristics of family groups, and not as individuals defined through occupation in societies where the division of labour is highly diversified; and,

3. Because their total number, or proportion of the population, in any nation state, is far too small.

A further reason is that those employed *directly* by the Rentier economy, e.g., venture capitalists, bankers, stock exchange employees, etc., are not necessarily ideologically committed to the purpose or outcome of their tasks, but only to their vested interests as individuals in earning a living. All this is to be contrasted sharply with the ideological commitment of the former bourgeoisie to the principles of capitalism in defensive opposition to any alternative system advanced by the proletariat.

8 – Why the new majority disdain class-based politics

Another impediment to raising the flag of class war is that the middle-middle majority are not psychologically inclined towards such political action for a raft of reasons. The first condition for class hatred is an underdog (or *Untertan*) mentality, and this is only achieved through a sense of helpless oppression by a remote elite one has no hope or wish to emulate. Such a hated class must represent cultural and other values to which there is total hostility. As the middle-middle majority possess the skills and qualities of the knowledge-based society, they are fearless and indomitable in the face of any sector of society. They have no reason for resentment, and they are deferential towards none. Through their aptitude and self-confidence they have made the world their oyster.

When they are faced with difficulties, which all encounter sometime during the course of life, they choose to act as individuals and not as a collectivity. The idea of drawing towards a comforting solidarity with its feeling of mutual support, would only fill them with a sense of shame and repulsion. This is because their pride as individuals ensures they take responsibility for their own fate, and choose to work for their own particular circumstances which they see as differing from that of others. They look towards ingenuity, legal loopholes, or clever talk in extricating themselves from a difficulty, and not to some over-arching generality to which they must submit.

A final reason for refraining from class-based politics, overt or merely implicit, of the middle-middle majority stems from their moral sensibilities. Difference is the right of all individuals, but toleration alone can stand as the guarantee for this. And difference is not necessarily a question of choice or eccentricity – although it often is – but more significantly, a matter of birth, nurture, or education. Is not a person entitled to an opinion and to express it freely according to the judgement which springs from his upbringing? We live in a society where discrimination is not made against those of a particular colour, race, nationality, creed, culture, gender, disability, or sexual orientation, and yet we live in a political system which maintains its existence through the greatest and most unfair discrimination of all, viz., through exploiting the differences of class.

Is the man or woman who speaks with a southern accent anymore blameworthy for that then the British citizen of African descent because of his black skin? The discrimination of the socialist is no less unjust and "racist" in its intention when he aims his barbs at the accent, the clothes, or the demeanour of the middle classes, than the street urchin who hurls abuse at the black man or the "Paki." The evil of socialist *racism* stems from the simple fact that accent, clothes, and demeanour, do not betray the character or convictions of those they purport to portray. Appearance is not reality, and only the ignorant believe it is so. Class-based discrimination is the greatest injustice of any category of discrimination for two reasons: firstly, because it is promoted by inference through the political system, and hence becomes acceptable; and secondly, because in terms of number, more people are openly subjected to this form of discrimination than any other.

The middle-middle majority sense this reality, but for the present it remains an unspoken truth. They therefore prefer, for the time being, to express their distaste for the political system by quietly withdrawing their support. But when politics has been transformed into a more pure form of democracy, men and women will look back in horror at the left/right divide, in the same way that they do at the wars of religion in the 16th and 17th centuries. When that day arrives, the person who launches an attack against one class or the other in attempting to foment division, will be arraigned for his inhumanity in a court of law as those who are presently charged for similar misdemeanours on racial grounds in our courts today.

9 – The universal economic issues of our time

In turning to the universal economic issues of our time in the advanced industrial economies, they will be found on examination to be no less unjust, oppressive, or outrageous to the interests of the majority, than those issues which oppressed that very different majority a hundred years ago. And yet the response of the new majority, for reasons partly elucidated, will be so different from that of the old.

But the day will come when the middle-middle majority will awaken to the consciousness of its strength and justified indignation, and respond with a suddenness in alarming the complacency of the establishment. The new middle-middle majority have many of the characteristics of the old middle class, and the latter were notorious from 1789 onwards and throughout the 19th century for revolutionary activity in promoting their own vested interests.

Picture-book histories, of course, convey a somewhat different impression, viz., that the working masses are the instruments for revolution, but before the 20th century the proletarian masses were no more than cannon fodder for the bourgeoisie, for it was the latter who derived all the benefits when quiet had once again settled over the land. The revolutions of the 20th century, on the other hand, although they were planned and conducted by those from a middle class background, were proven in the longer term to be of little benefit to any sector of society. This was firstly because power was transferred on ideological ground to those most ill-fitted to govern; and secondly, because the "dictatorship of the proletariat" was exactly what it purported to be, and hence socially oppressive to all locked within the frontiers of the nation state.

The middle-middle majority, however, do not anticipate creating a revolutionary situation, and neither is it necessary. When the hour arrives for change, they need only declare that "the emperor has no clothes," and everything will collapse at their feet before awaiting their enthronement. Their quiet self-confidence is derived from both their number and their monopoly of knowledge in all spheres of activity. It is only their heterogeneity and their present quiescence which projects them as a harmless mass to be used like clay in the hands of the political establishment, but when they do awake, their anger will be god-like and righteous, guided by a positive sense of direction. It will not be marked by the underdog resentment, or chaotic violence, or meaningless slogans, parroted by the proletariat in days gone by, but by a decisiveness and logic which brooks no contradiction.

These universal economic issues acting as a catalyst for change, may be listed as under: property values' inflation preventing the younger generation from ascending the first step of the housing ladder; student loans leading to ruinous debt; the long-term unemployment of highly qualified graduates, or their proletarianisation through packing supermarket shelves; and the impoverishment of the retired through the failure of the state to establish proper pension arrangements. The first three of these issues apply to the rising generation, whilst the fourth applies to those just now entering their retirement age.

10 – These issues are dismissed by the left as representing middle class "interests"

It may be asked, why is the Labour party, or equivalent movements, supposedly in the political forefront for social justice, in other advanced economies, so silent on these issues? The reasons are not far to seek, and may be listed as under:-

1. They have increased public debt through irresponsible borrowing and so are in no disposition to be philanthropic;
2. They have colluded with the forces of Rentier and transnational capitalism in undermining home-based industry, thereby increasing unemployment, particularly of highly-qualified occupations.
3. Through a misunderstanding of their ideological tradition, they have linked the purpose of internationalism with the worst aspects of global capitalism, ignoring the fact they

are politically powerless in the face of international capital;

4. Whilst claiming to support the cause of education, in Britain over the past decades, in collusion with a largely Marxist-driven academic elite, they have trashed all levels of the educational system; and,

5. Through their failure to understand the mechanics of Social Wealth Creation, or the financial-industrial system, they have felt obliged to renege on effective policies for reform in creating a more just and egalitarian society.

If the above statements convey an over-critical judgement of the left, it should be borne in mind that several purposes cited above were initiated by and are still pursued by the right, and so the above is also critical of the latter.

It should also be noted that despite the Labour party contradicting all its original ideals, in its two-faced situation, it nonetheless retains its bias in favour of the disappearing cloth-capped proletariat – even if this is not reciprocated as we observed in an earlier chapter. This means it has little sympathy for the middle-middle majority – the existence of which it fails to recognise. The left, because of its ideological stance which overrides the sociological reality of our time, only recognises the two classes bent on mutual destruction. Hence Labour has no ear for the pain of what it sees as the "middle" class, and maintains its disdain for middle class values even when its own leadership has sprung from such a background.

This is why Labour is silent on the usury which has led to property values' inflation, for socialists are not supposed to "own" private property. Instead the party is active in promoting the movement for extending Council housing – and I am not exaggerating when I say I am still bombarded with spam to support the cause of Council housing on an almost weekly basis. The extortionate system of student loans, and the impoverishment of those who have worked hardest in attaining their degrees, are other issues which fail to touch the heart of the Labour party. After all, only the privileged are believed to "chase after university degrees" – even though such an attitude clearly conflicts with the Labour party slogan of, "Education, education, education!"

The swindle of pension plans is another issue on which the Labour party is silent. Whilst company pension plans are now toppling off the horizon of most business enterprises as no longer economically viable, the Personal Pension plans, thought-up and organised by the great financial institutions are now being exposed as a worthless swindle when it comes to paying their beneficiaries. As for the old-age state pension, it is so minimal, that its dependents are made to live on little more than bread and jam, and disgracefully, are hardly able to meet their bills for heat and lighting.

In fairness, it has to be admitted that the Labour party – and the Tories and Liberal Democrats too – are so confused by the pensions problem, that they do not know in which direction to turn. The only sector of the population which "sits happy" in the light of the future, are our parliamentarians, the civil service, and the super-rich, with their enormous inflation-proof arrangements in enjoying an old age of superfluous wealth.

11 – The left is blind to injustice against the new majority

The absurdity of the left, through their entrapment in a time-warp of the past, is demonstrated through their literature passed around in their own narrow circles. This portrays the world of the 1950s rather than the 21st century. This is not to deny that pockets of extreme poverty still exist in Britain – and in America – and indeed, are increasing by the day, and that such problems are urgent and call for a high priority. The falsity of the vision, however, is that it paints a wrong impression of what oppresses the new majority. It is the latter which reflects the major socio-economic issues of our time.

As we have argued in an earlier chapter, in Britain the heterogeneous underclass or *Lumpenproletariat* may be estimated at 7 ½% of the population – few of which are prepared to support the Labour party or any other political movement. It therefore falls to top-down state authorities to rescue this wretched minority from its hapless condition. The major problems facing society today are those which confront the 90%+ majority – for the reason that they represent an overwhelming majority – and these problems can only be resolved though creating a uniquely new democratic system.

These problems are major – and worsening – and concern issues of social justice and egalitarianism to no lesser degree than the problems of the minority underclass. But the socio-economic problems of the middle-middle majority, as we have said, are met by the silence of all parliamentary parties, and to the best of my knowledge, of all other political groups. It must now be our task to address these questions and search for a road which will take us towards a better future.

CHAPTER 7
The unrepresented middle-middle majority is the political and democratic hope for the future

"Great achievements come to those who have learned to sacrifice themselves to the ideal which flashes before the inner eye of conscience."

S.R. Gardiner, *History of England 1603-1642*,
Longmans Green, 1886, Vol. VII, p. 53.

1 – Politics must be based on scientific realism   2 – The middle-middle majority as the political class of the future   3 – Why it is ideally situated in promoting full democracy and social justice   4 – Full democracy requires that financial power be made democratically accountable   5 – True democracy is conditional on the high educational standards of its people

1 – Politics must be based on scientific realism

If politics is not power it is nothing. Good ideas, howsoever well thought-out, or good intentions in themselves lead nowhere, except towards a turning inward, and inevitably a gradual retreat from worldly matters. Ideals can indeed be wrought into complex intellectual structures, and spiritually they may exert immense power over the minds and behaviour of humankind, but if they become divorced from terrestrial matters, they often lead towards a charismatic or religious rather than a political direction.

The irritants arising from the pain of want or oppression are the only motives towards large-scale human action, or organisation for change. If the power of an oppressor is so great that the population feels it cannot challenge established authority, then it may turn to religion as a last resort, as occurred in the Near East in the Roman Empire in the first centuries of our era, or in Russia following the invasion of the Mongols. If, on the other hand, a population has a political consciousness and the courage to challenge authority, it will resort to a political response entailing an appropriate degree of defiance. If it veers between the two situations indicated above, i.e., if a population is politically immature, it may resort to a utopian or charismatically-inclined style of politics which in the longer term tends to be impractical or self-destructive, as occurred in Russia in 1917, in China in 1950, and other territories in different epochs of history.

All those engaged in political activity – on however small a scale – should therefore seek to measure their impact, or eventual influence and power, on a realistic basis. They should avoid relying on fine phrases, or strong emotions, or empty promises, or good intentions of any kind, unless these things are based on the demonstration of facts. If they fail in this, they become ridiculous, or are dismissed as charlatans, or are considered by those in power, or with relevant knowledge of the ways of the world, to be people of little account. In launching new ideas for change the first consideration is that such ideas be scientific, that is, sociologically predictive and based on economic principles which in themselves change the nature of society.

If the latter is demonstrated with convincing arguments, it will arouse the alarm and anxiety of established authority. Attacking and defensive postures are thereby created, and without the need of formal organisation the population will naturally divide into one side or the other. In other words, politics should begin by identifying and pointing out the obvious and straightforward – even though the obvious is being communicated to the public for the very first time. This is the child's game of simply pointing out that the emperor has no clothes, and so exploding the myths and stupidity of the age.

Politics is the power of manipulating majorities through asserting their vested interests and explaining how these may be achieved. Politics is ruthless – even in the best governed communities – and its ethical justification is only based on a nice balance between the openness and integrity of its intentions in conjunction with the social acceptability of its methods. In advanced industrial economies the latter entails the call for effective democratic mechanisms.

2 – The middle-middle majority as the political class of the future

We have already identified the huge potential significance of the new and unrepresented middle-middle majority which has emerged over the past 60 years. This heterogeneous mass can only be described as a class because of its underlying but unifying socio-economic interests. In that alone can be found its reality as a class – or in any class. It is unrepresented because its existence is new and unprecedented, even though it was brought into existence over a period of time through a combination of parliamentary legislation and evolution in the world of work. None of the political parties in any advanced industrial economy *intended* to create the middle-middle majority.

They intended nothing more than the very abstract notion of creating a more democratic society, which they could imagine as amounting to little more than the raising of living standards. All politicians have their own vision of the world, and harbour in their hearts their own ideological desires, but none can foresee the consequences of their actions, or those of changing democracy – and why should they, for when was the future ever accurately predicted by those who live in the present? And a question of more significance: why should the politicians, to whom this new majority is deeply indebted for its benefits over the past 60 years, predict the creation of a class which would turn on and destroy their old and well-held ideological beliefs? The only satisfactory answer to this can be found in the Hegelian dialectic in that when two opposites clash they produce a synthesis quite different from the originating causes which brought them into being.

The middle-middle majority, in its present situation, could be described as a sleeping class. It lacks a self-consciousness and awaits its awakener, which will arrive through a combination of inevitable circumstances in conjunction with political design. We have described these circumstances above, viz., a usurious financial system barring home-ownership to the younger generation; the millstone of student debt – sufficient to raise ten thousand Raskolnikovs; and the collapse of a proper pensions system to support those about to enter the troubled waters of retirement. We have already noted those distinctive characteristics of the middle-middle majority which already mark it off from any previous class, viz., its toleration of difference and intolerance of intolerance; its feeling of vulnerability in a financially and environmentally unstable world; its isolation through individuation and through the broad diversification of occupations and leisure pursuits; and of course, its disdain and alienation from the political system.

Its existence is further emphasised by the evaporation of the old working class and that of the bourgeois values of the old middle class. Whilst the proletariat has been reduced to a fraction of its number through absorption into the middle-middle majority, the greater part of the old middle class has simply been transformed through the process of time and the force of circumstances, so that those now in their 60s and 70s have very different attitudes and viewpoints of the world compared with 50 years earlier. For one thing, they have foregone their pride and much of their self-confidence and sense of status. They are instead content to merge with the new majority, and enjoy a more private life even if materially bettered.

3 – Why it is ideally situated in promoting full democracy and social justice

The factor which above all signifies the power and potential of the middle-middle majority, is to be found in its monopoly of knowledge in all spheres of activity and learning. And in this is to be found the greatest promise for the future of humanity. If the middle-middle majority has not as yet awoken to the political consciousness of its vested interests, or if it is slow to do so, this could in part be due to the fact of its quiet self-confidence and freedom from that eroding resentment which so infected the discontented in the past. It is not in competition or conflict with any other sector of society, and it has nothing to fear from any human direction, although much to fear from a malign financial system and the threats of environmental catastrophe. It therefore feels – until the present time – that it is not under undue pressure to pursue its interests or disturb the quiescence of the status quo.

The greatest promise which the middle-middle majority holds out for the future of humanity is to be derived from the core of its ethical values, and this in turn will lead to the soundest and most true form of democracy which is yet to come into existence. These values stem from the centrist positioning of the middle-middle majority in representing the totality of all that is best in society. This can be understood through the fact that the old middle class was never *middle* in the correct sense. It occupied a superior position in society and recognised its identity in subordinating the working masses.

The new majority, on the other hand, recognise that it comprises a balanced mix between those across the entire spectrum of the population, and because it is unthreatened by the poles at either end (with their limited numbers) it is unhesitatingly prepared to acknowledge the practical principles of justice and egalitarianism in all their desirable forms. Whilst the classes of former epochs may have notionally acknowledged the values of democracy and social justice (in so far as their vested interests were not affected), it is only the middle-middle majority which feels a total commitment and obligation to fearlessly develop those values to their fullest extent. The latter will only come into being through realising the practicality for the first time of implementing *full democracy* within the nation state, and bringing this into actuality.

Democracy means nothing more nor less than people power. As an attractive idea it may be ventured and asserted by people anywhere on the planet, but its full realisation is only possible when majorities reach a sufficiently high level of both technical and general education. Whilst Technical education maintains the existence of advanced industrial economies, General education is concerned with an open information society whereby people may understand not merely the business of government but all the levers of real power – particularly in the financial sphere. Full democracy cannot be achieved through the limitations of representative systems – howsoever fair, well-organised, or free of corruption they may be.

4 – Full democracy requires that financial power be made democratically accountable

Representative systems are not only hindered by the blocking agencies of questionable filters, but the ideas and policies passed through such filters are liable to too broad an interpretation or distortion, and consequently, to resulting division amongst those who originally gave those ideas and policies their support. Representation may be expedient and convenient to organise, but it is unsatisfactory in achieving the wants of the ordinary individual who uses the political system. Casting an occasional vote on a 4-yearly basis is a very limiting form of power. This fact was first pointed out as a weakness of the English political system by Rousseau more than two hundred years ago.

Only *direct* democracy through the medium of referenda or plebiscites can hope to genuinely empower the ordinary individual, and only then can full democracy be realised. In the complex world in which we live today democratic mechanisms need to extend beyond the immediate concerns of government. This is because power which directly affects the lives of ordinary people, as we have noted, is something which extends far beyond the remit of central government as we experience it today. Hence government may install and maintain effective democratic mechanisms for all authority within its remit, whilst nonetheless the majority exist in a state of bondage in a nation which is not only undemocratic but rife with injustice and inequity.

This occurs, of course, when the financial-industrial system, international or otherwise, is not directly answerable to national government for all its activities. The role of democracy therefore needs to be extended to include those powerful institutions outside government control, i.e., to banks, corporations, and other transnational financial bodies. If this is not achieved then what is claimed to be democracy may be little more than a charade – especially if government is controlled by economic forces of which it has minimal know-how or little right to challenge. In the advanced industrialised world today it is not governments which are oppressive or tyrannical, but usurious institutions which overrule governments.

Hence those forms of power which intrude into all our lives, and the dichotomy of that power between governmental and non-governmental, needs to be recognised first if full democracy as a right is to be demanded by the majority. Some of the ways in which non-governmental authority may be democratised and brought within the dirigiste authority of the state in safeguarding the interests of the majority are listed as under:-

1. Through co-determination (*Mitbestimmung*) in all places of employment through differing systems according to the type and size of organisation.

2. Through employee share ownership and the control of enterprises, and their openness with regard to the earnings of all personnel, and management structure and promotion prospects, etc.

3. Through changes to Company law enabling the ownership and control of business to be extended to all sectors of personnel according to their competence, commitment, and share ownership.

4. Through ensuring that banks, stock exchanges, and other funding and financial institutions are democratically accountable to *external* inspection bodies, with power to intervene, control, initiate legislation, and remove directors and other officers as they see fit through their own tribunals open to the public.

5. Through reconstructing the Monopolies and Mergers Commission as a more powerful organisation, with an effective publicity department in engaging greater public participation.

The purpose of the above should be to bring all forms of financial power within the surveillance and intervention of the state in safeguarding the welfare of the public, but *not* under the direct control or management of the state.

5 – True democracy is conditional on the high educational standards of its people

None of the safeguards or benefits of full democracy are practicable without the presence of a highly educated majority, for the reason that those in all occupations, or other spheres of life, would be called upon to engage in democratic activity, i.e., in taking legal as well as moral responsibility for the management of society according to both their preparedness and the limits of their competence. No democracy (worthy of the name) can exist without the high intelligence of its people, and the democracy of ancient Greece was only enabled through the skills and creativity of majorities amongst competitive trading peoples. As responsibility is the correlative of democracy, it follows that when enterprises or public institutions are opened to the pro-active participation of their employees, efficiency is thereby tenfold increased.

The left have attempted to create the myth that democracy is for "ordinary people," and for people worldwide in resolving their differences. It is true that the abstract right exists – or is generally said to exist – for peoples to organise themselves as they wish. It is also true that when society reaches a certain evolutionary stage in its industrial development, the democratic mechanisms of the left/right divide is useful in advancing the causes of both progress and social justice. However, the establishment of a democratic *system* out of the blue, or its natural adoption during industrial development, does not necessarily reflect the existence of successful democratic government. These truths have been demonstrated clearly many times throughout the 20th century.

It would be a useful exercise to ask the relatives of African peoples raped, mutilated, or hacked to death, in almost any part of the sub-Saharan continent, if they believed in the "blessings" of democracy. It needs to be reiterated that the horrors of the anguish and suffering of the millions massacred or driven from their burning homes and villages in that unhappy continent, were all the victims of democracies granted as an *abstract right* which went awry. These are the evils which emerge from the good intentions of former imperial masters. It is my supposition that the answer to the above question, of those long-suffering people, would be along the lines of pleading, as might be the following: "God spare us from the chaos which democracy has brought, and bring us the justice and equity of strong government which springs from the wisdom of the knowledge-rich, and the benevolence of those who are better placed than ourselves in the art of government."

The American attitude – also shared by the UN and most of the world – that democracy should be imposed on all peoples under all circumstances at all times, in resolving their worst crises, is wildly wrong. In taking the situation of Iraq and Afghanistan at the present time, for example, attempts to impose democracy in these countries is not simply failing, but is an irritant whereby the chances of establishing *sound* democracy recede rather than progress. This is because, in such countries, there is no understanding or sympathy for democracy, or for the exchange of ideas or cooperation to make it practicable, and so corrupt and vicious practices are encouraged rather than discouraged, as the worst or most unscrupulous persons promote their own vested interests against the rest of the population.

This is the natural response of most tribal peoples to the imposition of unfamiliar political practices, and so the principles of democracy are contradicted through gun-law and bloodshed, and conflict is unnecessarily aroused where there was none before. What then is the answer? It is only to be found through the provisional imposition of authoritarian rule by the most educated secular leaders of goodwill committed to universal education and literacy, and a socially just and egalitarian society. Only after a period, as a new maturity develops, will the foundations then be laid for establishing long-term democracy on a secure basis. And a modern national consciousness, transcending tribal loyalties, is the most important foundation of all. No nation is created through declaring territorial boundaries alone, and European history has demonstrated the essential link between national consciousness and effective democracy.

The supposed gift of democracy is a poisoned chalice when passed to those who have not reached that sufficient level of civilisation to receive its blessings. Moral blame must therefore be passed onto those European post-War governments for their too hastily shaking off the responsibilities of imperial power. They were no doubt in part influenced by the prospect of bankruptcy after an exhausting war to continue the costs of colonial administration, but that is hardly an excuse for failing to pursue an educational blitz in the spheres of literature, philosophy, and the social sciences, in attempting to create a democratic consciousness. The granting of independence without the assurance of 100% literacy, and a love of scholarship amongst the general population, doomed such societies to a state of anarchy, the breakdown of the infrastructure, and eventual bloodshed.

Democracy is the best form of government, and it is the only system able to guarantee the individual the fulfilment of potential in terms of ability and the enjoyment of life, but it needs to be harnessed to promoting the aspirations of all through education and higher standards in all spheres of activity. And it is in these latter respects that the left, on one hand, and American civilisation on the other, have failed peoples throughout the four corners of our planet.

With these thoughts we must now turn to considering the relevance of the middle-middle majority in acting as an accidental catalyst in bringing about a form of civilisation which will be unique and better than all those in previous history.

CHAPTER 8
The profitable Productive economy must displace Rentier capitalism

"It has often been remarked that the countries which prove richest are those which are poorly endowed with natural wealth."

J.R. Seeley, *Life and Times of Stein*, CUP, 1878, Vol. I, p. 177.

1 – Democracy and individual freedom 2 – The state should be wary of ideology and charismatic tendencies in political life 3 – It should promote culture as the medium of communication 4 – Current failed attempts to break the political mould 5 – Futility of movements failing to confront the financial system 6 – The two forms of capitalism 7 – The greater socio-economic success of Productive over Rentier capitalism 8 – Britain's state of denial over her failing capitalism 9 – Why necessity will enforce Productive capitalism on a fragile world 10 – How the world lost faith in a benign America 11 – Political and industrial elites are everywhere in the pocket of America

1 – Democracy and individual freedom

It is not only the argument of this book that a just and equitable society within the framework of full democracy for achieving the greatest happiness of humankind should be sought on ethical grounds, but because in the longer term, it is the most effective means towards resolving the greatest problems on our planet as well as the most efficient means of government. The argument is therefore both moral and utilitarian.

Such conclusions could not be drawn with the certainty intended unless we had reached the present stage of technological development. Other cultures in less developed parts of the world may draw quite different conclusions on questions of government, human happiness, or ethics, but without wishing to draw the accusation of arrogance, this is due to their not having reached a sufficient level of understanding or consciousness on the nature of reality. In taking such a scientific approach to political questions, we are therefore repudiating the trends of post-modernist philosophy in claiming a degree of objectivity in our analysis and conclusions which most in the contemporary age may be reluctant to adopt.

An empirical stance should always be maintained, and the purpose of government is the good of the individual as an end in himself and not as an instrument for some other purpose. If this Kantian principle is observed, great caution is needed in discussing humankind as a political or social animal, particularly with regard to collectivities and assumed loyalties. In the first instance government should facilitate channels for the full intellectual, physical, and spiritual development of the individual within the framework of his personality, abilities, and inclinations, for these things equal the maximising of a person's freedom – or lead to that end.

It is assumed that the individual is freed from the immediate wants of food, shelter, clothing, and warmth, but government has a greater obligation to the individual than these. It should be the purpose of government to ensure the fulfilment of individual personality, and of course this is implied not only through an educational system, but through all legislation assisting the disadvantaged. Hence freedom *from* want may be a primary question for the state; but freedom *for* is the great question for all within any civilisation worth the name.

2 – The state should be wary of ideology and charismatic tendencies in political life

It should not be the function of the state to preach or teach ideologies of any kind which undermine rational thought through superstition, thereby threatening the freedom of individuals and society. The state should be wary of promoting any such sects or movements in safeguarding the precious plant of freedom requiring the constant vigilance and nurture of leading opinion-formers. This is argued in view of the fact that in those countries where charismatic movements are strong – irrespective of their cultural heritage – they are often adversely affected politically with regard to questions of social justice and equity, and this is traceable to non-rational modes of thinking which penetrate secular life.

America and India are two of the most prominent nation states to be cited in such a context. It is alleged that the Panglossian belief of the average American in that he lives "in the best of all possible worlds," could not be maintained unless his reasoning faculties had been badly unhinged by an excess of religious charisma. Whilst in America every vagrant imagines he is to be magically rescued from his plight through the ever-expanding "opportunities" of his country, so in India the impoverished masses remain contented in their condition thanks to the consolations of religion and the promise of eventual Nirvana.

It may be countered that although Americans and Indians may be contented peoples, despite all the injustice and inequity existing in their countries, it would be morally wrong to assert that contentment alone should be recognised as the criterion of the well-governed society. Apart from the subsidiary question of defining or measuring contentment in any particular society, there is the more important question of truth understood in terms of objective reality. In the medieval world – and still today in many non-Western and non-Confucian societies – it was held as morally acceptable to deem a society as sufficiently self-fulfilled, irrespective of humiliating deprivation, if its people collectively were upheld by religious faith. This was usually on the grounds that material conditions in the present world are of little account, and what only really matters is the hereafter.

To the modern, post-Reformation, or humanist mind, such an attitude is not only utterly repulsive but grossly immoral. It is immoral on the general grounds that people are material or physical beings, and should live their lives through the exercise of these qualities, for if on the contrary, they attempt to live their lives as *purely* spiritual beings in *denying* their physicality, they enter into a false consciousness in repudiating and self-harming an essential part of their being. This may be illustrated through the particular example of the hard-working American head-of-household who passively accepts to be driven penniless with his family by bailiffs onto the street as an "act of God for his sins," whilst failing even to ask himself as to whether he has been wronged as a human being.

It also applies to the young hard-working American, who is struck down by a curable form of cancer for which he is unable to pay the treatment, who happily accepts approaching death "as the will of God," without even asking himself as to whether there could exist the possibility of a health service or the financial wherewithal to save his life. The usual psychological response of the American to poverty has always been "shame," or self-blame, but there are circumstances in life when even shame is an immoral reaction. And this is when the individual fails in his sense of sociality, or belonging as a member of society, when conditions may exist which are so intolerable, that no person should be made to bear them.

In the face of such conditions, therefore, a misdirected sense of shame entails a withdrawal of social responsibility from considering the needs of humanity. If a person is prepared to accept passively a gross act of injustice inflicted against himself, he will certainly not be sympathetic towards others in the same situation, and even less will he be prepared to act politically for the common good. Such examples may, of course, be illustrated with more acuity in India, where mothers gouge out the eyes of their infants, or cut the tendons of their thighs in supposedly preparing their children for a more successful career as beggars. In the recent blockbuster, *Slumdog Millionaire*, there is a character who narrowly escapes the first example of these horrific common practices.

Both America and India are societies with extremes of wealth and want, and both portray the evil outcome of superfluous wealth alongside grinding poverty, and the obscenity of uncaring and immoral attitudes which arise from this. In neither country is there a social conscience which drives their political sense towards the need for reform, for whilst in America politics is driven by a selfish individualism, in India it is driven by the demands of the caste system – even though this contradicts the constitution of the country. But in both countries it is only through the excess of religious feeling, when the heart takes over from the mind, that the social conscience is excluded from political thinking as a source for practical action.

In Europe or the Far East, any country which tolerated such injustice or atrocities as cited above would justifiably be ashamed of describing itself as a democracy, and yet India is constantly boasting of its status as "the *largest* democracy in the world." Meanwhile, that other country steeped in charismatic and false values, is constantly reminding the world it is "the *greatest* democracy on earth." Both countries may display outward forms of democracy, but the truth is that neither have the true spirit of democracy in promoting the best aspirations of humanity, nor do they practice it in advancing majority needs. It is no coincidence that the country with the highest proportion of regular churchgoers in all Europe, is not only the country which has promoted the bloodiest strife between different religions, but is also the most intolerant of racial and other minorities. That country is Northern Ireland. And the reason for this is only to be found in that excess of religious *enthusiasm* (to use an established 18th century term) which smothers the rational ability to differentiate between right and wrong.

The above is not intended to diminish the better function of the churches, nor even as a slight on the general purpose of religion. In well-balanced societies, e.g., throughout Western Europe, the churches serve as a significant social bonding mechanism in the community. Furthermore, religion is part of the human psyche, and although its degree may differ from one individual to another, it is psychologically ineradicable. Hubris and disaster would be invited on the human race if, for example, with the emergence of the new majority and its mutation into the knowledge-based Responsible Society as the egalitarian totality of humankind and absolute masters of the planet, this was to coincide with the refutation of the deity. Such a fall would deservedly follow from the existence of such unjustified pride.

Nonetheless, religion may become a malady in society, the obvious symptoms of which are those devious thought patterns, promoting prejudice or bias in blocking the successful resolution to serious issues. The best response to religion if it occurs as a pathological condition in society is not the promotion of atheism, as advocated by several leading thinkers today, for such an approach is futile, but rather through advocating Deism, or religion without revelation. This is the truthful approach to religion as well as the most respectful approach go God in the contemporary scientific age. It also acts as a convenient stepping stone in communicating with religious or semi-religious bodies or individuals influential in the spheres of political life or commerce. For example, in openly expressing my candid assent to the existence of an impersonal One-God who works without the need for partners, I have always retained the respect of business friends in Saudi Arabia, although in deference to Islamic theology, I have chosen to refrain from outlining the nature of the Deistic God. I might tentatively suggest, in this context, that readers consult my book, *Deism and Social Ethics*, for a discussion of such international issues of our time.

3 – It should promote culture as the medium of communication

Whilst the state should refrain from ideology, it should safeguard and actively promote the culture of the nation state or the civilisation within which it exists. This is not primarily because of the value of culture or its artefacts *per se*, but because it remains an essential source of communication between individuals and amongst communities, not only in terms of language, but of feelings, modes of expression, and the spirituality of art, music, etc. Culture marks the identity of a society in the same way that personality marks the identity of the individual.

Without the unifying power of language, there could be no development of the intellect or exchange of ideas. An integrated, well-balanced, and happy society cannot exist without a strong culture, and this is why it must be the priority of every nation state to safeguard and promote its own distinctive way of life, and especially to ensure that high culture is brought to the majority. We now live in a world where the cultures of all peoples are threatened and this is a threat which never existed in earlier times. This is an urgent topic to which we shall return below. The promotion of culture by the state is clearly correlative to promoting the freedom of its people.

The above is a thumbnail sketch for achieving the just and stable world desirable for our future. We shall demonstrate how it is a vision to be realised through the political medium of the middle-middle majority. But before such a world may be built there is a hindrance to be confronted and defeated. This is the evil of Rentier and global capitalism.

4 – Current failed attempts to break the political mould

The theory and practice of Productive or Social capitalism is the socio-economic system fulfilling the interests of the middle-middle majority, and the needs of all humanity. This socio-economic system and its implications for the future of humankind are described in depth in my book, *Social Capitalism in Theory and Practice*, and what follows below is a necessary summary of the principles so that the argument of this book may be comprehended and continued in its proper context.

Over the past 150 years until the present time political life has been divided between the interests of capitalism and those of socialism, or variations thereof, but all included somewhere within the conflictual left/right spectrum. Recently, in view of the realisation by many that our democratic political system is becoming increasingly creaky, other political theories have emerged in an attempt to break the political mould. For example, there is the left Communitarianism of the philosopher, Charles Taylor, inspired by such figures of the left as Raymond Williams and R.H. Tawney, and their influence is expressed through the imaginative Labour MP, Jon Cruddas; the academic Jonathan Rutherford; and the Chair of Compass, Neal Lawson. There is the left Republicanism of the historian and former Labour MP, David Marquand, the political influence of which is latent in organisations such as London Citizens.

Turning to the opposite wing, there is the right Communitarianism of Karl Polanyi, author of, *The Great Transformation*, and Phillip Blond, at one time advocate of the Progreesive Conservatism project at Demos, and later a member of the new "Red Tory" think tank. Other supporters are David Green and Anastasia de Waal at Civitas, and the former Conservative leader, Iain Duncan Smith. Then there is the centre Republicanism of Philip Collins, a leader writer for *The Times* and former speech writer to Tony Blair; Richard Reeves, director of Demos; James Purnell, whose theory of "power egalitarianism" develops a number of civic themes; and lastly, Amartya Sen, with his interesting ideas on the equality of "capability."

These leading alternative political visions for change are concerned with such admirable concepts as "solidarity and mutuality," the "dispersal of power," "the good society," "restructuring the state in a more decentralised direction," "political and economic localism," and "enabling a wider distribution of assets," etc., but they all lack the most important approach of all. None are concerned with the central problem which impinges on all others: viz., the financial-industrial system and the need for its transformation in serving the interests of all.

5 – Futility of movements failing to confront the financial system

This is where the socio-economic system of Productive capitalism differs from all other political philosophies in grappling with the major issues of our time. In contrast to other political groups, it does not shy away from issues on account of their challenging dimensions, but confronts them in recognising the necessity to do so. Anything less than the call for the reconstruction of our financial institutions at once diminishes any political movement intent on the public good to futile time-wasting effort.

Until the present time capitalism and socialism have been conceived politically as at the opposite ends of the spectrum, which is a stymied view of attempting to understand reality, and consequently, adherents of both ideologies have tended to misunderstand one another as well as themselves. The adherents of capitalism in the Anglo-Saxon world put all trust in laissez-faire (letting things be) and the invisible Hand, for the beneficent outcome of their system; whilst socialism repudiates the idea of the market, and places its trust in redistribution through state intervention, whilst turning a blind eye to the needs of the business dynamic. Again, in the Anglo-Saxon world, both conflicting groups tend to recognise capitalism as a single-type system: viz., as a Rentier money-making machine with the rationale of maximising shareholders' profits.

Those on the right support this concept since it is simplistic and serves to avoid controversy or further explanation; and those on the left support the restraining definition in condemning capitalism outright, and in upholding their argument that no other forms of capitalism could conceivably exist. This, of course, is very helpful in maintaining polarised left/right political positions. It is also helpful in ensuring intellectual stupidity on both sides of the argument.

6 – The two forms of capitalism

A more realistic understanding of capitalism, as demonstrated through its historical development, is the recognition of its bifurcation into two distinctive types: Rentier and Productive. Rentier capitalism is characterised in the Anglo-Saxon economies and most of the developing world. In terms of modern history, i.e., from the time of the industrial revolution, it may be termed the *original* form of capitalism, in its emphasis on money markets, international trade, and freedom to operate unhampered by government interference. Productive capitalism, in the same modern era, is only traceable from the latter half of the 19th century in Continental Europe and Japan – and later amongst the other Far East Tigers.

It is typified by extensive state intervention in regard to technical education, the establishment of industrial investment credit banks and similar institutions, state subsidies for manufacturing industry, and selective protectionism. Its leading theoretical proponent in Northern Europe was Friedrich List. Historically, Productive capitalism arose as a necessary defensive response to the crushing competitiveness of British industry, at a time in history when the complexity and costs of plant had become too high for family savings, or failed to attract sufficient investment capital from existing institutions. Hence business was forced to turn to the state for assistance, whilst the state in its turn was only too happy to oblige prospective industrialists in building the strength of national economies.

If that is the historical explanation, it is only in the decades following the Second World War, that their pattern as benign and malign forms of capitalism clearly emerged through comparison. And such differences did not arise through intended planning, or the aims of government, or the quirks of cultural influence. There is no evidence that industrialists in either the Productive or Rentier economies were any more or less benevolent or mean-spirited then the other. The differences therefore arose through the intrinsic characteristics of the systems themselves, and hence we uncover the same patterns of success in West Germany, Sweden, and the Netherlands, as in such contrasting cultures as Japan, Korea, or Singapore.

Let us look at these comparisons by first glancing at the malign Rentier economies which should have enjoyed every advantage as the victors of a world war. The micro-economic view of enterprise reveals under-investment, antiquated plant, poor management, failure to penetrate markets or maintain competition, and the worst labour relations known to history. The macro-economic view reveals the polarisation of wealth between rich and poor, low wages, relatively few consumer goods due to low productivity, sluggish innovation, and poor morale throughout most occupations – even though at the same time living standards were soaring, and this in turn led to a deadening complacency.

7 – The greater socio-economic success of Productive over Rentier capitalism

The underlying explanation for the above failure to perform effectively stemmed from a usurious financial situation, more interested in passive than active assets (i.e., land and property as opposed to primary or secondary industries); the rationale defining the purpose of business as maximising investors' returns rather than producing goods and services for the broader population; and the *total* absence of appropriate institutions for funding industry long term at low rates of interest. The City was virtually divorced from home-based industry, since it was geared to promoting the international trade of an Empire it had lost, but in the post-War period it quickly and effectively reorganised as a wider world centre for financial markets.

If we turn to the benign Productive economies, on the micro-economic level we discover enterprises from the very small to the large, enabled to borrow unlimited amounts for establishing profitable and expanding businesses from appropriate credit industrial banks; effective democratic-style management in charge of modern plant; and excellent labour relations due to good wages; the shopfloor involvement in management decisions; and employee share ownership schemes. This in conjunction with high morale and surging productivity led to the rapid capture of foreign markets.

On the macro-economic scale it led everywhere to diminishing average differential earnings between higher and lower pay rates, a wider distribution of consumer goods in raising material standards, better and higher pension arrangements, and more egalitarian and socially just societies in alignment with the democratic ideal. Again, these benefits stemmed from the nature of the financial system which succeeded in keeping usurious activity at bay through the purpose of productivity recognised as a socially desirable end.

8 – Britain's state of denial over her failing capitalism

It is regrettable that this significant bifurcation of capitalism throughout the Western world was rarely brought to public notice. One reason might have been the greater economic divide between the East/West power blocs with the concentration on the polarisation of views which this entailed. A second reason may simply have been pure ignorance of the real situation. A third may have been the natural complacency which arose from relative economic growth in choosing to turn a blind eye to the more significant international comparisons with competitors. A fourth and more significant reason might have been the hyper-sensitivity of bankers and financiers in the US and Britain, not merely to criticism but to any discussion of the established Rentier model. Many City financiers – as well as those in New York – have been quick in their anger to deny that the Productive model could be described as "capitalism." But if it is not capitalism, then what is it?

This state of denial that an alternative capitalist system ever existed has been disastrous to the Anglo-Saxon economies, for through the competitive *free market* system, it has led *directly* to the widespread destruction of manufacturing in both Britain and America. Had there arisen in good time, amongst leading industrialists, a consciousness that there was a better method of funding industry or modernising plant, then Britain and America need never have plunged into economic decline. I well remember when serving in the Army in the mid-1950s, there was a Welsh civilian clerk employed at our camp who constantly expatiated on the so-called German "miracle." He had recently returned from a posting in that country, and elaborated on the high living standards enjoyed there, and that smoke "with every colour of the rainbow" poured from the forest of factory chimneys in the Ruhrgebiet. We soldiers, sitting in the NAAFI, listened politely to his over-awed accounts of this "eldorado," but behind his back, we mocked and laughed at what we believed was his incredulity, impersonated his idiosyncratic Welshness, and said he must be "lying."

Some three years later I visited Germany for the first time, expecting to encounter a hard-working people, but still burdened by hardship and poverty. Ruins and bomb sites there were aplenty, but almost on arrival, on descending the train at Cologne, I was astonished by the prosperity and optimism of the people; the shops stuffed with luxury goods – at that time still unavailable in England; and by the restaurants and cafés offering a quality and variety of cuisine unseen in tumble-down Britain which had only recently discontinued rationing. I was also impressed by the egalitarianism of a country apparently without class barriers, and that cigar smoking which in Britain was not even enjoyed by the middle classes (except at Christmas), was there indulged in by railway workers as with their hammers they tapped the wheels of railway carriages.

As evidence of the few tourists visiting the country at that time, I obtained a ticket at short notice for the Bayreuth festival which today has a 10-year waiting list, and after attending a performance of *Parsifal*, I even secured a personal introduction to the young Wolfgang Wagner, grandson of the composer, who within several years, on the death of his brother, Wieland, was to become the longest running administrator of the theatre. As soon as I landed back in England, as with many others, my bags were rummaged through by eagle-eyed customs officials, and to my dismay I had to pay a hefty duty on various photographic odds and ends purchased abroad.

At that time, as a young man, I was still innocent of the world of finance and its nefarious methods, and could not explain the reason for West Germany's prosperity and economic strength. The reason, of course, was that she flourished under a Productive capitalist system and was free from usury.

9 – Why necessity will enforce Productive capitalism on a fragile world

But now in business circles in the 21st century there is developing an awareness of lost opportunities, and the realisation that past ignorance and complacency has been the cause of all our woes. The Productive or Social Capitalism of the future, however, does not entail reproducing an exact copy of that system in those happy decades following the post-War period. For one thing, the system varied from one country to another, and more significantly, we have moved ahead and have new problems to encounter. Furthermore, it is not contended that any one Productive system reached perfection. The real lesson to be learned is the experience of benefits enjoyed in so many different nation states, by comparison with the miserable inefficiency, waste, social injustice and inequity of the Rentier capitalistic model.

The problems of climate warming, together with other environmental issues, are likely to change the direction of economic policies everywhere in the near future. Huge public works will need to be constructed, and it is unlikely that the free markets of Rentier capitalism are capable of raising the financial resources needed. These projects will be capital intensive as well as labour intensive, and major initiatives will need to be directed by the state. Meanwhile, the habitual attitude of business in increasing productivity as an end or virtue in itself will call for serious review. Already in the eyes of the thinking public such an attitude is met by scepticism in the light of varied environmental issues.

Consumerism, waste, and the ills of unnecessary obsolescence is already polluting and poisoning the planet. What sense is there in productivity if its only benefits are employment-giving or the production of useless, throwaway baubles? The culture of the future will necessarily be less acquisitive and more contemplative: i.e., it will be more concerned with the enjoyment of those things of permanent value, as family relationships and the cultivation of friendship, and will encourage a greater absorption with the arts and world of learning in better understanding ourselves and the nature of existence.

Nonetheless, in view of the urgent crises in the decades ahead, productivity is likely to be more important tomorrow than it is today, but greater discretion will be necessary as to how we utilise our industrial muscle. And certainly the principles of Productive capitalism will need to be called upon as the Rentier system is consigned to the dustbin of history. Funding will be raised through differing methods of deficit financing through responsible lending institutions established for the purpose, as opposed to resorting to the stock exchange equities of the open markets with their unreliability and the consequent millstone of usurious debt. Deficit financing may indeed be partly long-term low interest debt-based, but it may also be debt-free when linked to careful administrative arrangements.

10 – How the world lost faith in a benign America

The ills of Rentier capitalism have been many times increased through the political power situation now pertaining in the world. In the immediate post-War period there was optimism in the world and great hope for the future, and this was reflected in the attitude and spirit of young people at that time, compared with the deep pessimism and alienation typical amongst young people today. This is not intended to cast a slight on the character of young people today, for they have every reason to mistrust those who have bought the world to its present sorry plight.

In the immediate post-War period America was regarded politically as a benign international influence. The Bretton Woods institutions had been recently established by academics and leading economists to help create more just and equitable conditions for the peoples of our planet, and there was no suspicion that any of these good intentions would go awry. But the optimism was short lived. The greed and cunning of American bankers, financiers, and corporate interests, soon penetrated the great international organisations for global reconstruction, and through the instruments of extortionate usury, turned them into the fly-traps of destructive debt. No sane person today, for example, could describe the World Bank or the IMF as anything other than organisations which have brought the misery of poverty, hunger, and national bankruptcy to peoples throughout the Third world.

The wretchedness of Rentier and global capitalism was not to become a worldwide phenomenon amongst the advanced economies until a somewhat later period, i.e., the 1990s, first in Japan and the Far East, followed quickly afterwards in Continental Europe. There was no holding back the eventual conquest by American financial imperialism – even in countries which hitherto had safeguarded their industries and national integrity. The tempting buying power of the transnationals could not be resisted by those in leading positions, and when local industry was compromised and then made insolvent, it was too late to fight a rearguard action.

11 – Political and industrial elites are everywhere in the pocket of America

The situation today, as we have said, is that the political establishment of no advanced economy is prepared to challenge globalisation and this is on the grounds that it is too difficult to do so. But it should be borne in mind that political establishments, and the leaders of parliamentary parties across the spectrum, are either directly or indirectly in the pockets of American interests. The pretence is often made that global interests are purely international, and this is given as a "do nothing excuse," but such a simplistic contention is quite untrue. America is unquestionably, both politically and economically, the most powerful nation of our age, and Neo-liberalism is her ruling ideology which ensures that globalisation should be promoted as a *right* as well as a *might*. Meanwhile, establishment politicians, leading civil servants, and industrialists of other advanced economies are not merely bought up as the pawns of American power, but more significantly, are cushioned by inflation-proof pensions, and earnings on a scale which far transcends that of the 97½%+ majority.

It may also be asked: how many of the above in leading positions own second homes in America, and to what extent does this affect their loyalty to their own peoples? For all these reasons, added to the comforts of security and wealth, there is no motivation or inclination for change of any sort to the status quo. Affluence soon turns our politicians into stage actors where all differences are just "academic." And as they anyway remain powerless in most situations, why should they worry their heads about the outcome of any decision-making?

CHAPTER 9
The knowledge-based new majority as the foundation stone for a just and equitable world

"Truth lies not on the substratum, but as the wisdom of the ages bears testimony, in a well, which only those who will take the trouble of digging deeply can find, although it be easy enough to draw when once the sealed-up fountain has been discovered and opened. ... Expediency! Perish the word, if guilt be covered and moral justice sacrificed to such considerations!"

Agnes Strickland, Preface to, *Lives of the Queens of England*, Colburn & Co., 1851, Vol. I, p. xi.

1- Time for the new majority to bid for power 2 – How the left/right divide and not left or right views *per se* frustrate political progress 3 – Emerging new values of the middle-middle majority 4 – A balanced perspective of working life 5 – Egalitarianism in the knowledge-based society 6 – The new majority enables high culture as the standard for egalitarianism 7 – Conflicting ethical values on cultural standards 8 – Those vested interests in suppressing standards 9 – Vested interests of the new majority in promoting standards

1 – Time for the new majority to bid for power

The entrenched power of the establishment and its immediate servants, living as they do in stability and affluence, with an attitude that "Alls well with the world" is the grim reality facing us today. But there is one sector of the population which is concerned about the future: not that tiny minority at the apex of society, and not that hopeless underclass at its base, but the huge 90%+ majority in the middle.

It is only the middle-middle majority which is passionately concerned for change, so that their children and grandchildren may ascend the bottom rung of the property ladder; that the rights of property be restored as *personal* possession, and not as the possession of corporations or the state; that pensions equivalent to two-thirds of final earnings be made available to all by the age of 70; and most urgently, that effective measures be taken to meet the challenge of climate change.

The failure of political establishments everywhere to recognise – let alone act – to counter the greatest social and environmental problems of our time is not only symptomatic of their moral and intellectual bankruptcy, but of the collapse of democracy itself. This will be the judgement of history. Its proof is demonstrated through the total break between the will of the majority and those who purport to govern. To the horror of those who exist for a past which is gone forever, the golden rope of fate woven by the Norns has fallen apart, and a new light appears in the dawn. Now is the era for the new majority to ascend the throne of power.

This heterogeneous mass of the population, which in the eyes of demographers assessing people power, may represent the totality of the population in any nation state, will discover its identity through both its subjective vested interests and broader responsibilities in saving the planet; and it will discover its power and confidence for action through its monopoly of knowledge. But first this majority needs to repudiate the existing political system on the grounds of its unworkability in achieving further good for humankind; and also to repudiate the conflicting left/right ideologies which in a former epoch resolved issues, but now in their diseased state only compounds them.

2 – How the left/right divide and not left or right views *per se* frustrate political progress

What does this political critique exactly entail? It does not mean that ideas or policies stemming from either the left or right are necessarily wrong or malign in themselves. Often policies floated from the far left are admirable, as also are those from the far right – if indeed they properly fit such categories in the first place. The only criterion for a policy is not whether it conveniently fits the ideological Procrustean bed, but whether it is apt or good in itself as legislation for majority or minority needs within society. In parliaments in all advanced industrial economies may be found outstanding politicians from every sector of the political spectrum. Their place in that spectrum does not in itself begin to define their competence or good judgement.

It might also be noted that politicians of the left sometimes advocate policies of the right and vice versa, and their opinions are none the worse for that. But because of the conflictual nature of our political system, we live in a society where labels stick. Consequently, it is common practice nowadays that politicians criticise those on the opposing benches irrespective of what they have to say on the principle they belong to the opposition. An example of this, which may be cited, occurred recently when the allegedly right wing Mayor of London, Boris Johnson, floated the praiseworthy policy of implementing an experimental free cycle use scheme modelled on that in Paris for Islington. This environmentally friendly proposal for exercising the good citizens of the borough was savagely attacked by the left wing councillors of Islington on the grounds, I would argue, that anything proposed by Boris Johnson should be opposed on principle.

A somewhat different situation arose recently when Tony Woodley, General Secretary of the Unite union, attacked the government of Angela Merkel in allegedly buying off Canadian decision-makers to preserve German-based car plants, on the grounds it was upsetting the "level playing field" as to where manufacturing bases should be retained or shut down. This is an absurd attitude for a British trades union leader to take, and does nothing to save British jobs.

It may be asked: what is meant by a "level playing field" in this context? It means playing along with the current principles of globalisation and remaining a poodle to transnational American interests. The German government – as indeed with any other Continental European government – traditionally protects its industry against external threats. Britain *never* does so in the cause of what is described as "free market principles," which in reality means surrendering to international capital as a first priority. If Tony Woodley wished to serve the best interests of his workers, he should ignore the left/right politics of the establishment, repudiate globalisation, and openly fight the cause for home-based industry as do our neighbours across the Channel.

These may be minor instances of the counter-productive influence of our political system. The real critique of our political system in its degeneration is not to be found in the opinions which men and women may hold, but rather in the loss of the underlying ideological foundations supporting either left or right wing views. This is because it has led inevitably to a falsity of outlook, or an artificial standpoint in situations when criticism is made. All this reflects, of course, insincerity and hypocrisy. The problem arises through the transformation of society and the world of work over the past 60 years in creating a new reality. This means that the ideological perspective of politicians has slipped into a time-warp of the past, and they are reduced to advancing a fiction.

The end result of this process is poor quality legislation, or worse still, legislation and addenda piled on top of each other which compound rather than resolve problems for the longer term. These tendencies are most clearly brought to the attention of those who have engaged in political life at any level of the system. Perhaps it is most clearly revealed at the grass roots level of political discussion by any party branch of any constituency in the country. It is marked by an overall impression of unreality and disconnection from the *Zeitgeist* of the contemporary world.

3 – Emerging new values of the middle-middle majority

The middle-middle majority through its unique characteristics, which mark it out as a class quite different from any other in previous history, will accordingly emerge with a political *Weltanschauung* reflecting its vested interests and viewpoints of reality. It is also extraordinarily fortunate for humanity that because of its 90%+ majority, it is not confronted by any other opposing sector of significance, and hence it is fearless in facing issues with unprecedented objectivity and confidence. This also signifies it will unhesitatingly pursue the cause of social justice and equity with commitment as a natural consequence of its intrinsic character. It would be unable to act otherwise.

The first emotive response of this new majority will necessarily be a rejection of the left/right perspective, as otherwise it would be unable to advance to the next step of constructive thinking. In a world where there exists humankind but no classes, there is naturally no need or opportunity to think in terms of class interests. All that remains is to comprehend humankind from a disinterested sociological viewpoint. Firstly, one turns to the psychology of the individual in identifying needs for his full development, and then to social groups and their interactions, and the role of culture as a medium for communication, nurture, and education.

As the priorities of social justice, equality of opportunity, and egalitarianism, are always borne in mind, the best needs of the majority plus the special needs of minorities are served most effectively. In such an ethical and intellectual environment, the idea of class divisiveness in diverting or twisting the discussion of substantive issues is hardly allowed to occur. If it was allowed to occur, the outcome of best practical policies would be frustrated or blocked.

The middle-middle majority, and through its awakening consciousness, its mutation into the Responsible Society, will entail the emergence of new ethical values in conjunction with the evolution of humanity, and the consequences changing social conditions. All these will arise as an inevitable outcome of the evaporation of class differences and conflict. The individual in his striving for success and financial accumulation in meeting the costs and responsibilities of family life, will seek to pursue his interests as a virtue in itself, since thereby such activity would not seem to compromise the interests or welfare of other individuals or sectors of society.

4 – A balanced perspective of working life

The saving and accumulation of capital, providing it does not exceed the superfluous, will be regarded as laudable in its contribution to total wealth through taxation and expenditure into the community. The ethical justification for the accumulation of wealth, or earnings of any kind, would rely on the fact that it is accrued through labour and not through usurious arrangements deemed contrary to the principles of Social Wealth Creation. The above tendencies in regard to the sagacity of the individual's self-interest would be complemented by the social qualities of magnanimity towards the less advantaged, and commitment in serving the community. These qualities would be encouraged by two factors. The first would be the ubiquity of democratic life and the honours which would need to be conferred in holding public office.

In a society where *direct* democracy is prioritised over representative systems, and is enabled to replace the latter whenever that is practicable, there will emerge a natural democratic mindset and sense of obligation to serve the state as the higher form of expression in carrying out the will of the individual. In this way will arise a political consciousness similar to that in the democracies of ancient Greece, which are the only notable *direct* democracies to be identified in any earlier civilisation. Due to the technology of the time, such democracies were restricted to the *polis* or nation state not exceeding an average of 3,000 citizens. In the 21st century, on the other hand, with the help of information technology, there is now no limitation to the population numbers of the nation state in facilitating *direct* democracy – being the only effective basis for people power.

The second factor would be a more temperate business environment which relaxes the intensity of competition, and certainly ends the senseless striving to ever-greater productivity which leads to needless imbalances in the economy. Business and productivity are necessarily the first priorities in any nation state, but they need to be kept within the framework of a culture with a broader vision of life than the mere pursuit of Mammon. The baseness of American life stems from the pursuit of this, and its consequent ills, and all other values become a faint disguise for the pursuit of money. This is the reason why American culture must be prevented from dominating the world, and why American values should be rooted out and subjugated wherever they threaten to upset natural human relationships. A major function of civilisation and high culture is to present a balanced perspective of life, which directs the mind of the individual towards self-understanding and an understanding of the world we live in.

In practice this means that the individual should not see himself, or be seen, primarily as an engineer, a doctor, or a lawyer, but as a whole person with a rounded personality, who seeks to achieve goodness in his attitudes and actions. Perhaps the best book in helping the individual to achieve a balanced and virtuous life is still *The Nichomachean Ethics* of Aristotle. Although there may be some aspects of this book which are not entirely relevant for our time, the underlying themes remain apt as a basis for the morality of the Responsible Society. It is true that commentators over the years have expressed reservations on this book in that it lacks heart or passion, but since it is concerned with *social ethics* and correct behaviour and relationships (and not the perturbations of the soul) this is a specious criticism.

The soundness of social ethics is not to be found through the intuitional feelings of the heart or the excitation of the mind, which leads to the irresponsibility of mood swings, but rather by turning to cool judgement through the use of reason. This is asserted despite the fact of the greatest philosopher of the Athens of the North declaring we are all "the slaves of our passions," since finally, in all decision-making we are obliged to remain dependent on the tool of reason in striving to achieve good judgement and sound action.

5 – Egalitarianism in the knowledge-based society

A people freed from the shackles of class struggle, standing confident and true to their individual identity, need to be liberated from religious influences encouraging a slave morality. This is because it leads to a herd-like collectivism, and this in turn soon culminates in oppression. This matter is touched upon because the heritage of the left has been driven by a false mentality identifying oppression as in itself a right to resentment and hostility against the powerful, the knowledgeable, or the good, and of course such feelings or attitudes cannot be justified on those grounds alone. This is because they lead inescapably to the suppression of standards, and an anti-intellectualism giving feelings a higher value than the tranquillity of thought, and ultimately to the self-destructiveness of resentment as a psychological mindset.

In the real world this is best illustrated through the Labour party's interpretation of the *New Testament's* moral entreaty that, "the first shall come last, and the last shall come first," in that the "good" are the underclass whilst the "bad" are represented by the higher echelons of society. In Labour party and socialist thinking worldwide, this means that the individual should not be judged according to his personal characteristics but rather according to his or her class or appointed authority within the community. When put into practice this leads to examples of the grossest acts of injustice as we have seen in Eastern Europe and further afield in the 20th century.

As for the idea that possession is "corrupting," or that a person should donate his property and all his worldly goods to the poor, although it may be attractive to the slave morality of those who have nothing, it contradicts every notion of prudence for the individual's self-regard for himself and his family. On one occasion I have seen such religiously-motivated advice put into practice by a professional couple, and it led to the break-up of good relationships with their children as they were left without the wherewithal to complete their higher education. Such irresponsible advice could only be given by single persons existing on charity at a leisurely pace of life in a sunny clime. I have elsewhere argued at some length that the possession of property is a necessary condition for the full development of the personality and a successful life, and this totally contradicts the commonly repeated Christian message.

In Britain today, the "first shall come last" or slave morality is also interpreted in another light. Hence we live in a society where old age pensioners are arrested and prosecuted by the police for punching burglars who have broken into their homes, whilst the courts release the latter without punishment. Teachers with long and impeccable records are sacked and stripped of their careers on a single incident of manhandling unruly pupils creating classroom mayhem. House owners who retaliate against feral kids who tear up their gardens and smash their windows are punished for assault, whilst those guilty of criminal damaged walk away laughing from the courts on receiving their "badge of honour" with ASBOS (i.e. Anti-Social Behaviour Orders).

Whilst hardened criminals receive derisory sentences, those guilty of minor offences are viciously punished by the courts – if they belong to the middle classes or have a blameless record. Murderers and rapists are released within a decade of their offences, to murder and rape again – which they often do. Most recently, and widely publicised, was the case of a mother and disabled daughter who committed suicide following many years of persecution and assault from a gang of youths. Despite many complaints to different authorities, no action was taken to defend the rights of this defenceless couple, and whilst the perpetrators remain free to live out their wicked lives, the mother and daughter took their's through the desperation of suffering.

All these decisions of authority may have been inspired by the slave morality of the Christian message, but in the *real* world they make for increasing chaos, instability and injustice throughout every level of society. Is it any wonder that crime rates are soaring by the day, when those who would prevent crime, or act as good citizens, are deterred by the fear of prosecution?

A slave morality weakens rather than strengthens the ultimate intentions of those who so identify their position in relationship to a stronger adversary. Those who choose to see themselves as an underclass and use that as a subtle weapon of hostility, quickly transform themselves into tyrants and enslavers when the time is ripe. History has demonstrated this many times in the last hundred years alone. This is not intended as a criticism of the established churches, but it is intended as criticism of that fundamentalist Christianity which has so impaired the attitudes of the left, and more recently, in another context, in the USA, the attitudes of the right.

A society without class divisions must aspire to egalitarianism, and the latter calls for a nice balance between equality and liberty. But an egalitarianism of the knowledge-based majority demands not simply the availability of high culture for the many, but its actual absorption through an educational system in encouraging upward mobility, and a society allowing for downward ability without loss of status – or at least loss of face. Such societies already exist in the Far North and in certain territories of the Far East, but they are dependent on strong cultures, and widespread involvement in high culture, with regard to either its creation or appreciation.

6 – The new majority enables high culture as the standard for egalitarianism

It should be noted that the idea of high culture in which the majority are deeply absorbed, is something which has not been previously achieved in Western civilisation – and indeed has been repudiated as impractical in academic circles from the time of Plato almost until the present. The reason given has always been the same: viz., the old aristocratic (or snobbish, by today's interpretation) of the necessary class divisions of society into the incapable, uneducated, or stupid lowers orders, in contrast to the intelligent and enlightened upper echelons.

Educational institutions worldwide, through the persistence of traditional prejudice, still in great part hold to these ideas, despite having modernised attitudes in other areas.

But today with the emergence of the new majority, there is no reason why the struggle to achieve the reality of an egalitarian society should not be pursued through the transformation of school education in extending the joys and benefits of high culture to *all* our children without exception. Resistance to the success of such a policy, however, needs to be anticipated from the start. The money-making media would exploit not merely the youth of the world, but all sectors of the population, in debasing the taste and sensibility of the majority in all spheres of leisure activity from eating out to listening to music. This is because those things which are most basic, simplistic, or superficial, or tend to excite the senses rather than feed the cognitive responses of the mind, have always attracted that majority which is less curious for knowledge or less inclined towards its acquisition, and hence this offers a greater opportunity for easy money quickly earned.

Those business people who unscrupulously exploit the natural weaknesses of people for their own profit, would therefore prefer to market the Rolling Stones rather than Hindemith, or Dan Brown than Proust, or McDonalds than the fine cuisine of a reputable chef.

7 – Conflicting ethical values on cultural standards

The question needs to be raised as to the morality of this. In the Christian tradition there is no intrinsic virtue in intelligence, as virtue is primarily defined as refraining from sin, and because of this, the debasing of taste or sensibility is not sufficient to arouse the moral ire of the religiously inclined. In the classical world, on the contrary, there is perceived a virtue in intelligence and in all good creativity.

Knowledge, in the eyes of the Christian has always been suspect since the first apple was plucked from its tree, and subconsciously this attitude is still cherished by the left-leaning underclass in their hatred of the powerful. This is illustrated by the fact that Labour party branches are always happy to welcome the least educated and unskilled into their midst, but are suspicious of anyone with a higher education or who seems to betray an intelligence somewhat above the average. Such people are held as being *morally* suspect in that they might have right wing leanings. What hope is there for a party which is guided by such a criterion of right and wrong?

Medieval Christian tradition had a special place in its heart for the mentally deficient, and as late as the 19th century, the village idiot in Russia was held in special awe as "God's anointed." In the struggle to maintain cultural standards, this is yet another reason for turning to the ethical values of the Greeks in resolving contemporary issues. It is not suggested that the religion of the established churches of today be repudiated, but rather be regarded with silent reservation, and that whilst revealed religion should be neither honoured nor dishonoured, a more sincere adherence be given to the rational God of Deistic belief as being more in harmony with the intelligence and aspirations of people in the Third millennium. I have elsewhere drawn attention to the wisdom of Confucius when he heeded that "the spirits should be respected but kept at a distance." In other words humankind should concentrate its concern on the present world and not be too distracted by the irrelevance of the unknown hereafter.

In the eyes of contemporary society, those who market or are in any way involved in encouraging the debasement of good taste, or better sensibility, are therefore not judged to be guilty of wrongdoing. If challenged, their defence would be that they act in the name of their own freedom, and for the freedom of those who have a right to enjoy what they offer. But neither of these responses is truly valid for freedom may be used as an excuse for any action desired. No society endorses the freedom to murder or steal, but little over a century ago, there was still the freedom to supply and sell opium, laudanum, and other harmful opiates to the public. Over the centuries innumerable freedoms, once taken for granted, such as bear-baiting, cock or dog-fighting, have subsequently been made illegal on the grounds of their social unacceptability. It is our contention that in a more enlightened future age, through the increasing authority of the Responsible Society, that the debasement of taste and sensibility will become ever-more unacceptable, and that consequently the majority will voluntarily refrain from polluting themselves, in the same way that today's majority shun brothels, drunkenness, or smoking.

8 – Those vested interests in suppressing standards

The aggressive style of American business in maximising easy profits within the shortest term, is uniquely geared to degrading quality and producing kitsch whenever the opportunity occurs, and the question needs to be asked, how can teachers and artists worldwide counter such an influence which undermines educational standards? The short answer is only through exposing to ridicule American art forms and intentions, and by pointing out that high culture can never hope to survive as a healthy plant in societies so polarised between the very rich and the very poor. Furthermore, the poor are more easily manipulated to serve the interests of the powerful when their sensibility and intelligence has been polluted and corrupted by the populism of mind-destroying and usually passive activities. This is a theme I have explained in some depth in my book, *Populism Against Progress.*

In a class divided society, where the wealthy fear the eventual loss of their power and assets to an underclass, the former have a vested interest in suppressing the general educational standards of the latter. Misinformation is then substituted for reality, whilst sufficiently time-consuming addictive mind-numbing leisure pursuits are financed and supported, in ensuring that the lower orders have neither the opportunity nor inclination to examine the serpentine ways in which power is wielded by the elite. And this is especially the case in a country like America, which on the one hand purports to be "classless," whilst on the other is more polarised in terms of rich and poor than any other advanced industrial economy on the planet.

The above is not only an argument for upholding intellectual and cultural standards throughout all sectors of society, but seeks to demonstrate that the maintenance of such standards is an essential component for the kind of egalitarianism desirable for the future. The fear of egalitarian tendencies in the past has always been they drag down the standards of the higher echelons of society to a greater degree than they succeed in raising the underclass, and this has certainly been true in the recent past. With the emergence of the new majority or the Responsible Society, as the only political class of significance, the above apprehensions become irrelevant.

9 – Vested interests of the new majority in promoting standards

The Responsible Society will through its own volition and consolidation seek to maintain the highest cultural standards for all. It will have a vested interest to do so, for as relatives look to the future of the rising generation, they will strive to ensure their offspring meet their highest potential, and if for any reason they fail to meet the expectations of the older generations, they do not want their children to lose status or face, and sink irretrievably into the disgrace of nonentity.

But in a necessarily competitive world, it is not possible for all to fully meet their academic or career expectations, and for these there must be a safety net for their self-regard and dignity. In the future that safety net will in great part be found in the bonds and companionship of high culture in preserving the egalitarianism and inclusion of all. And these benefits will mark off the new civilisation in a unique way from all those that have preceded it in history.

CHAPTER 10
The Rationale for the Full Democracy of the future

"Since the monetary question directly impacts all areas of human activity, in order to make real progress towards justice, a clean environment, a sound energy policy, decent health care and retirement systems, and greater real freedom of choice and action for the citizenry requires the monetary problem to be addressed and solved first."

Stephen Zarlenga, *The Lost Science of Money*, AMI, NY. 2002, p. 2.

1 – Productive Profitability as the dialectic for democratic struggle

This leads us to the question of democratic mechanisms. As noted in Chapter 2, a democratic system is unworkable unless it is linked to underlying but realistic dichotomies between economic vested interest groups. But such divisions need not be class-based. Invented or assumed differences between different sectors in society, or those which are not based on economic interests in founding new democratic states, are, as we have noted in an earlier chapter, doomed to failure, and soon lead either to artificial or unnecessary conflict, or to the unworkability of government.

On the other hand, in mature multi-party states it may be observed that many democratic groups are seemingly cultural, e.g., in representing language interest groups, or alternatively, they may be occupational in representing agricultural or urban interests, but in examining such parties and the systems within which they operate, it will usually be found that economic interests underpin their practical utility.

What, then, is to replace the left/right democratic divide which has typified political life worldwide since the start of the industrial revolution? For an answer, we can only turn to the mechanisms of the financial-industrial system, and the desirability of Productive capitalism replacing the ills of the usurious Rentier economy. In this is to be found the new reality, and for its practical success, it is essential it be locked into a system of working democracy. In this way our economic ills, and the corruption and greed of bankers, financiers, and other money-lenders will be confronted and excluded through the organised and popular will of the majority. Democracy will stand with vigilance as a constant guard at the gates of the financial system, on the one hand promoting socially wealth creating productivity, and on the other, safeguarding against the tendencies of Rentier activity.

This would be achieved through promoting the principle of *Productive Profitability*, or Social Wealth Creation, as a desirable rationale in all socio-economic decision-making throughout political and business life. It would be opposed by the principle of *Rentier Profitability*, or Unsocial Wealth Creation. The rationale would be applied throughout all levels in the workplace or in political life, in deciding objectively best policy for the public good. Its purpose would be to promote productivity through minimising cost; through reducing or eliminating the charging of interest; and to maximise the benefits of productivity as generally beneficial, rather than tending to exclusively serve the interests of those different sectors responsible for productivity.

In an open discussion situation, irrespective of whether it would be concerned with marketing or planning or with labour relations, all would be asked to eschew personal vested interests in favour of the enterprise or organisation, in the belief that the ultimate success of the latter equals the longer term success of all those committed to its success. In such a discussion, all would be equal and subordinated before this single over-arching purpose embracing the better interests of all. Senior executives no less than junior employees would hence be called upon to consider the end purpose or greater good of the enterprise above their own particular vested interests or occupational involvement in the company, and in this way all parties would strive to achieve sound and objective decision-making. The rationale sought would always be through the question, "Does this contribute to the true best productive long-term purpose of the organisation; or does it on the contrary sacrifice the purpose to Rentier or usurious interests which drain the financial or other sources of the organisation?"

Hence Productive Profitability favours the making of profit – even the maximising of profits – whilst being deeply concerned with the use to which profit should be allocated. The advancement of the longer term against the shorter term is clearly intended to combat the ills of usury in its many guises and forms of deceit. In priority order the uses of profit should be:-

1. The payment of salaries to employees and directors;
2. The re-payment of expenses arising from running costs;
3. The re-payment of debt to credit investment industrial banks;
4. Reinvestment for product innovation, updating plans, and marketing;
5. The payment of taxes
6. The payment of employee shareholders' annual dividends;
7. The payment of returns to shareholders who are neither directors nor employees of the company, and such shareholders should be forbidden by law from exerting any executive powers over the company; and,
8. Other purposes, e.g., charitable, which the employees of a company may vote to support.

The rationale of Productive Profitability, however, would extend beyond the consideration of profit-maximising enterprises. It could be extended to the public sector where its benefits may be no less considerable in cutting back waste, over-employment, and especially parasitic self-generating legislation in keeping civil servants unnecessarily in their jobs. In this sphere inspection bodies would need be established in assessing tendencies towards the expansion of unnecessary bureaucracy, or over-employment, with authority to re-plan and downsize departments.

The principle of Productive Profitability would therefore be placed at the gateway of the *real* economy, in examining the credentials of those representing the interests of the *phony* economy, and cutting them down to size, or even excluding them as the occasion arises. This calls for a new approach to economic thinking, but never has this been more urgent than it is today. This is reflected in the words of the political academic, Andrew Gamble, when he wrote, "there has been much unfavourable comment on how little the contemporary economics profession has had to say about this new crisis. The events of the real economy have long since ceased to interest most economists."[12] In the same article, in referring to what I would term the Rentier economy, Gamble continues, "the greater the role of finance in the modern economy, the more unstable the economy is likely to be, and a key role of the state is, therefore, to find ways to build trust by creating greater stability." But such trust can only be found through nothing less than transforming the financial-industrial infrastructure into a Productive system.

2 – Full democracy achieved through the Responsible Society

Democratisation in the workplace, as well as in many other spheres of activity, is already fast advancing throughout the industrialised world, but there is still considerable need for changing Company law, as well as employment law, and the law of miscellaneous employing institutions, in giving greater teeth to democratic effectiveness. Notional or theoretical rights are

---

[12] Andrew Gamble, "Prophet Warning," *New Statesman,* 7th September 2009.

not sufficient in themselves. They must be practical and *practised*, not merely as rights but in promoting greater efficiency throughout the commonweal. Democracy is not to be promoted as a principle in itself – indeed it would be inexpedient to do so – but in meeting the expectations and abilities of the middle-middle majority as it awakens to its consciousness as a class and mutates into the Responsible Society.

The arrival of the Responsible Society entails the ownership and management of the means of production, distribution, and the means of exchange by the majority, not as a collectivity howsoever envisaged, but as *individuals*. In a society not divided by conflicting class interests there are no Haves and Have-nots in the sense of reflecting justice or injustice, since both ownership and control is equalised out amongst the totality of the population in so far as that is practicable. As there would be no sources for justified resentment on grounds of oppression from any sector of the population, all would seek to maximise the prosperity and success of their employing concerns as those with equal rights in proportion to their abilities and effort.

Whilst the vestiges of party or representative systems may still exist, greater power would be expressed through the *direct* democracy of functional groups in all spheres of activity, besides those of employment and politics – but the most significant functional groups of all, would be those which control financial power. And the latter would be situated in so many strategic positions, thereby presenting checks and counter-checks to every transaction, that usury would be minimised if not eliminated from commercial life. In these ways the virtues of democracy would be brought to their fullest possible development.

3 - An end to class war politics

At the start of this book we remarked on the difficulty – if not the impossibility – of imagining a political world devoid of the left/right conflictual divide. If we attempt to describe the purpose of such a political environment, free from the debasing influences of class prejudice, we may come nearer to understanding its benefits. Every aspect of the left/right divide is aimed at arousing bad emotional feelings, not through accident but through design. This is because it is intended to appeal to our most subjective vested interests, or selfish desires, usually through the arousal of fear or anger, for such methods are the most effective for a politician, promoting any cause, in attracting the greatest number of followers.

This, of course, is demagoguery – an accusation of which any politician would be ashamed – but in any society where the classes are engaged in a desperate struggle for political dominance, it remains the stuff of political life. But the tools of demagoguery, in all their intensity, are hardly less common in any democracy divided by deep-seated economic interest groups. Political struggle on such a basis cannot but be subjective as it appeals to the more questionable qualities of human nature, and has little compunction in exploiting deceit, hypocrisy, and the advocacy of policies which in any event will hurt the interests of some sector of the population.

But worse than that is the time-wasting and energy involved in such a struggle with its circuitous ways and deviation from the central purpose of resolving substantive issues. There is only one good purpose of political activity, and that is not so much the resolution of differences or conflicts between varying groups (for these are superficial questions reflecting deeper undercurrents) as the resolution of substantive problems lying at the heart or root of every conflict.

But the real critique of the effectiveness of the left/right divide, as we have argued in earlier chapters, is that it is no longer workable in advancing progress. With regard to recent history, this is most clearly illustrated by the violent policy swings following a change of government. The fall of Callaghan's Labour government in 1979 was not merely succeeded by a change of party but by an administration that reacted violently against every aspect of one-nation Toryism, even though that previous Tory government of Ted Heath had failed miserably in its attempt to unite the nation. After 18 years of disastrous Tory government, this was followed not by a reaction, or even a change of direction, as evidently desired by those who expressed their wishes through the ballot box, but by a further 12 years of Thatcherism continued by Labour rule.

We see here that the dialectic of democratic progress (i.e., of thesis, antithesis, synthesis) has failed entirely, which it had not done previous to the 1960s. That is, not only had violent change undermined the long-term economic interests of the country, but brought regression in the sphere of social reform. And worse still, not only had a change of administration brought *bad government* by any objective standards, but the betrayal of voters' *real* wishes in 1997 with the election of a Labour government which made no real changes with regard to what *really* mattered. In the words of Alice Mahon, quoted earlier in this book, "a cuckoo in the Labour nest" had been elected as premier. All this contradicts the purpose of democracy.

And now with the emergence of the new majority and the Responsible Society an entirely new situation has arisen. There are now no grounds for conflict between classes or large population groups. There is now no reason for politicians to arouse the warlike tendencies which may lie hidden within their followers' hearts. In the advanced industrial economies of the world, humanity has reached a sufficient level of maturity to view the future and the questions of the day, with analytical insight, informed judgement, and cool objectivity.

In the security of his knowledge-rich environment, he need no longer ask him- or herself the narrow question, "Does this fit my interests,?" but rather the broader question, "Does this suit the interests of my community, or the greater fellowship of humankind,?" in the confidence that the latter is also best suited to fulfilling his personal interests and those of his nearest and dearest. And more significantly still will be the way he examines and assesses policy proposals, which whilst they may not excite the senses will quietly satisfy the moral sensibility, as he weighs the many facts to be considered, adopts an academic approach in viewing issues, and finally reaches his conclusions in a disinterested frame of mind.

If the above sounds fanciful, then perhaps I should add it is based on personal observation and experience in the Far North, more than 40 years ago. In a series of articles published in a learned journal (and subsequently in my book, *Land of The Olympians*), I made an in-depth comparison between the calm political mindset of neutral Scandinavians as contrasted with the war-torn excitability of those entangled in the Russo-American conflict of the Cold War. If the Cold War is taken as a metaphor for the class struggle, the neutral Scandinavians may be taken as those who had already reached the evolutionary level of the Responsible Society by the early 1960s.

The maturity of the Responsible Society, now emerging everywhere throughout the advanced industrial world, is therefore a world of social peace with mutual respect amongst all sectors of society. A society which is free of class divisions and class conflict, and views problems in the light of their independent substantive existence, rather than as representing sectorial interests, will resolve issues with greater thoroughness and speed; will more effectively express the national will of its people; and enjoy an environment of greater harmony and contentment. Just as neutral Scandinavians, in that post-War period could look down with disdain, and a certain superiority, on those peoples who were so foolish as to embroil themselves in the losses and destruction of a world war, so the middle-middle majorities of the leading industrialised countries will look down in disdain on those peoples who continue to maintain the left/right political divide.

It has therefore become morally imperative that the pattern of class war democracy be finally repudiated by those seriously committed to political activity, and that such a pattern be replaced by the more realistic democratic system of Productive Profitability, so that financial power may everywhere be included within the remit of governmental democracy. And Social Capitalism, which will carry forward the practical implications of Productive Profitability, comprises a socio-political and economic philosophy appealing equally to all those of goodwill and integrity across the entire spectrum of parliamentary life. But in repudiating all preconceptions of the left/right mindset, a huge cultural shift needs to be achieved. Men and women will need to forgo the very concept that ideas or policies could be interpreted as either left wing or right wing, for such labels only obfuscate the reality of issues through attaching irrelevant and confusing associations.

In this way discussion is diverted from the substantive to the nebulous, for such associations refer to concepts which are out-dated or no longer credible or helpful towards the cause of constructive thinking. Old concepts and theories must be ditched, as new generalisations and principles take their place in matching the realities of our time. It is a certainty that if politicians are ever to regain our respect, then that is the road they must follow. The new intellectual vistas which such a road has to offer for the development of thought and practical action are immense in taking humanity across the frontier from one epoch of history to another. But none of this may be achieved unless we are prepared to repudiate the intellectual constructs of the past and undertake a revaluation of all values.

The above describes the practical ideal for a prosperous and stable society serving majority needs, but it will be of little avail unless political steps are envisaged for its achievement.

4 – Practical approach in confronting Rentier capitalism and its Neo-liberal ideology

Social capitalism would need to be organised not as a party, for that presents yet another prospective divisive element into political life, but rather as a loose movement of committed members meeting as *Circles* in one another's homes to discuss the ultimate principles for social justice and equity, and how it may be attained. Social Capitalists could fall into two categories: those who refrained from involvement with other political groups, to be known as *Independents*, and those who joined the established parliamentary party of their choice, to be known as *Political Activists*. The purpose of the latter would be firstly to penetrate parliamentary groups in propagating the principles of Social capitalism, so as to appeal to both the membership and leadership of the parties; and secondly, to point out the bankruptcy of the confrontational system and the futility of the left/right divide for any good purpose. The direct purpose of Social Capitalists working within the established order would be to strive for the cause of effective coalition government.

The larger scale political approach calls for the description of a more detailed strategy. An international organisation may be apt as a useful publicity tool, but as with most such bodies, its influence would be limited in achieving realistic results – especially when it is borne in mind that the purpose is to confront the most powerful economic ideology on earth, protected and promoted by the most powerful nation state. Neo-liberalism is the sacrosanct religion of Rentier capitalism, not merely of the American elite, but in their ignorance and false consciousness, of the masses.

Rentier capitalism is hardly less inviolable to the average American than is Mohammad to the Islamic believer, or Jesus Christ to the borne again evangelist. To many millions in the North American continent Rentier capitalism has become a superstition defying rational belief, and those who deny the faith are at once tarnished as the dupes of socialism. Change may yet follow in the wake of present misfortune, but as yet there is little to betray such a course of events, but for the sake of America and her sanity, it is hoped her people will awaken to the truth of the fate which must await them in the coming future.

But until there is a change of direction, America will stand as the threatening challenge to the rest of the world. It seems that she alone is the barrier to social justice and greater egalitarianism in so many territories around our planet. What then can be done to free the oppressed and impoverished of the world? As noted above, if politics is not concerned with power it is nothing, and so care must be taken to ensure that such a challenge does not descend into the complacency of a glorious but ineffective publicity campaign, or into a charismatic movement of like-minded people whose only achievement is mutual encouragement amongst themselves.

In launching a political challenge, it is necessary to be sufficiently candid in identifying and declaring the source of hostility before choosing the first move on the chessboard. An opponent in the struggle for survival should never be portrayed as an inexplicable force – as possibly something nebulous or abstract – unless it is the lunatic in the asylum struggling with his delusions. It must necessarily be concrete and clearly identifiable for all to see, with a trail which is traceable from its source directly to the individual who is struck by its hurt.

5 – Strategy required in challenging globalisation

This is the situation with the ubiquitous power of transnational Rentier capitalism, conceived and developed in its present form exclusively in America in its multifarious variations, and then exported worldwide as a usurious poison in destroying the hopes, happiness, and prosperity of peoples. Never since the days of imperial Rome has the world been faced with the prospect of both political and economic oppression on such a scale. The question has to be asked: in the apparent face of such crushing power, is the world to subside hopelessly into the fatuity of other-worldly religion (which is still a distinct possibility even in the 21st century) as a last resort, as happened then; or is it to use its rational sense and the world of knowledge in fighting back with a constructive alternative? The answer has to be the latter.

But glancing at the governments of the world at the present time, it is evident that few are inclined even to raise a hand in a defensive gesture. All points towards a fatal acceptance, although many in leading positions have already taken their thirty pieces of silver in sacrificing the interests of the many. But now in the 21st century the knowledge-based majority is armed and sufficiently competent to fight back. If the impending struggle was merely a question of defence, there might be doubt about the advisability of throwing down the gauntlet, but it is not the only issue. The greater concern of the impending struggle is not defence against injuries past or future, but a practical cause for the reconstruction of the world for greater social justice and equity.

For many reasons the practical or constructive aspects of the struggle can only be pursued within nation states, and through the cooperation of like-minded states for a common purpose. The necessary politico-economic changes to be achieved are many and complex, requiring a step-by-step approach in overcoming unexpected legal, commercial, and other international hindrances. The primary purpose of all nation states is clearly the maximising of their self-sustainability for safeguarding:-

1. All aspects of their economic and cultural integrity;
2. Their independence of foreign interference for whatever reason;
3. Their peoples, or any sector thereof, from financial or imperialist exploitation;
4. The institutions of democracy, and their effectiveness in promoting people power; and,
5. The protection of manufactures, and the profits derived from primary and tertiary industries.

It should be remembered that no country can be free or independent where international economic power is allowed to override the power of national governments, as we find throughout the world today. The old American slogan that "Commerce brings freedom and prosperity," has now become a sick joke. This is because commerce needs to be mutual if it is to be beneficial, i.e., it needs to represent an equality of exchange between peoples, and this it no longer is. Globalisation has turned trade into a highly exploitative activity, conducted by transnational corporations, often with offshore tax havens, utilising many financially usurious mechanisms in bolstering their profits. Furthermore, as we have noted, they are totally unaccountable to any external controls or authority, or evade those which would inspect or otherwise intervene in their business activity.

6 – Collapse of home-based productivity equals insolvency

The crisis facing the highly populated advanced industrial economies of the world is consequently both dire and urgent. This is because few countries can survive for the longer term without a strong base in producing tangibles, although smaller population countries may prosper through such primary industries as forestry, fishing, agriculture – or even mining. But globalisation over the past 20 years has put national trade in many countries so completely out of kilter as to threaten bankruptcy in the near future – and the tendency is accelerating with little comment in the world press.

A voice of protest, however, has been raised from an unexpected quarter. The City Minister, Lord Myners, in an interview in the financial section of *The Guardian*, pointed out that, "too many British companies are at risk of falling into foreign hands because their shares are owned by international funds unconcerned with their domestic heritage. ... We need to be alert to the fact that our share registers are increasingly no longer British. They are global and we have the most open market in the world for corporate control. All things being equal it is easier to take over a company here than anywhere else in the world. ... If the love of money is our defining purpose then we develop people who lack a hinterland and societies which are fragile."[13]

Much has been written in the past about Britain's manufacturing industry slipping down the drain, but productivity is now fast disappearing in the agricultural sector also. On the day I write these words the NFU has predicted that within ten years our milk industry will have vanished. Meanwhile, many food products marked "British" in our superstores are in fact sourced from overseas territories, whilst many vegetables and fruits which could be produced in the UK are imported from as far afield as Africa or South America. Such trade patterns are not simply madness but suicidal. They

---

[13] Jill Treanor, "Too many UK firms fall into foreign hands, warns crusading Myners," *The Guardian*, 24th September 2009.

may be profitable to transnational corporations, but they are disastrous to ourselves, as well as to the peoples from whom they originate as cash crops, who lose their land as self-sustainable peasants, and are pushed as a workless proletariat into mega-city slums.

The complacency in maintaining our own high living standards is upheld through our trust in the financial profits of the City – or at least, it was until yesterday. Tomorrow may be another story. It may be true that the international profits of the City of London currently represent 40% of GDP, but this is predominantly money paid into the Treasury, not into the community. Whilst the attractiveness of such a percentage seems to hold our government in thrall, if not in a blackmailer's grip – especially a government which is heavily in debt – it should also be borne in mind that our profitable financial services could fly out of the window overnight.

There is no reason why a country which now produces so few tangibles should continue to host one of the major financial markets of the world. Major financial centres have always tended to re-locate to those areas where manufacturing is strongest. Just as in the past we sustained the illusion we should *never* lose our competitiveness in producing motor bikes or white goods, so now we should adopt a more realistic view of the prospects of the City. In assessing the fragility and craziness of the financial markets, the future for Britain is therefore not so much vulnerable as unthinkable. This is the extent of the present crisis. It calls for action – and action now.

7 – Restoring home-based industry through appropriate legislation

The first step of nation states must therefore be to introduce a highly strategic system of selective protectionism, which whilst favouring friendly states, would be extended from year to year. The purpose of such a policy would not merely be the reduction of public debt or the enrichment of the majority, but steps towards greater economic self-sustainability, as well as the diminution of unnecessary or wasteful trade in polluting the environment with a gargantuan carbon footprint.

Meanwhile, home-based industries would be identified for protection, and other spheres of manufacturing or productivity would be marked for restoration or establishing on a first-time basis. Industrial investment credit banks would need to be founded in funding and financially monitoring such enterprises, but as such financial institutions have never existed in Britain, expertise would need to be drawn from elsewhere.

These institutions would sidestep or operate independently of the City, and to complement their activities, national stock exchanges would be established for the sole purpose of financing home-based productivity. Again, such stock exchanges would be very different from those of London or New York, in that they could be modelled along the discreet lines of the Swiss bourse. Dealings would be restricted to the authorised newly established or reformed banks, and only securities officially introduced could be dealt in; the banks working on commission and technically responsible as principals even when representing third parties; and business would be transacted daily between members by direct negotiation without jobbers or their equivalents being employed.

Whilst positive measures, as above, would be taken to build a strong-based employment-giving productive sector, other measures would be taken to counter Rentier or other exploitative activity, in sucking the life-blood from the nation state. Transnational corporations, irrespective of their place of registration or central office, would be subject to state-directed accountancy inspection at their own cost, with respect to assessing the financial benefits or disbenefits to the country in which they operate. Share-ownership and management control, within the relevant territory, would require a minimum of 51% in the hands of local nationals.

Meanwhile, conglomerates would be broken up into their constituent parts, in this way restoring home-based plants to their former independence. Their share structures or financial management would then be transferred to the newly formed industrial credit banks, and from then onwards they would be enabled to grow and flourish as Productive capitalist enterprises, in more effectively serving the interests of employees, consumers, and the national economy. Wherever possible independents would be converted into sole proprietorships or partnerships, and limited liability law would be changed in removing share-ownership proportions as the financial upper limit responsibility of directors. The latter would thus collectively incur total personal responsibility for company debts, firstly, in ensuring their full commitment and care to the management of the company; and secondly, in discouraging fraudulent practices, particularly with regard to opening insolvent businesses under other names. The latter has now become a major problem of creditors in Britain and elsewhere.

8 – Restoring home-based agriculture

At the same time a land survey would examine ownership patterns in both urban and rural areas throughout the national state. In urban areas a policy of freehold *personalisation* would be pursued in the sphere of domestic property. That is, housing would become the personal property of occupants, in minimising landlordism, although the demand for rental property would be fulfilled in satisfying the needs of short-term lettings. The term *personalisation* is used to define property owned by individuals in distinguishing it from the broader term *privatisation*, or from the third alternative of public property.

The ownership of land is perhaps the most sensitive property issue of all in any nation state. Agricultural land should be removed from foreign ownership or control, as also from that of corporations of any kind. Mansions or other property with restricted acreages of parkland, may be owned for the private use of embassies or visa holding foreigners providing no business use is made from same. Agricultural, forestry, and low-lying mountain areas, should be divided into commercially viable estates for the personal freehold ownership and working of family units. Such properties should be granted licence, for their assigned productive purpose, exclusively to nationals, as inheritable and inalienable from the state. In the event of the expiry of a line, or owners wishing to surrender their rights and move elsewhere in changing their occupation, the state would sponsor a suitable replacement family who would need to be examined by a local board of the NFU and church leaders as to their fitness and good character before being admitted into the community.

In maximising agricultural productivity and encouraging import substitution, the reintroduction of the Corn laws could be in the forefront of legislation, in promoting all sectors of mixed and organic farming. In areas with poor soil, or in such sectors as horticulture, labour intensive methods would need to be employed, but in advanced industrial societies such employment conditions are unlikely to be attractive unless, firstly, inherited landownership is established; and secondly, that the state is competent in ensuring profitable markets through removing usurious agencies between producers and consumers which have robbed the former of his rightful profits for so long a period. Only in these ways may the self-sustainability of nation states be best maintained.

9 – The Nationality principle essential for promoting home-based productivity

The above proposals for reform in eliminating Rentier business practices wherever they may linger, and replacing these with the fair and equitable principles of Productive capitalism, are intended for worldwide application irrespective of the level of industrial development. The above may have been presented through the prism of British or European conditions, but they are no less applicable as matters of policy for India, Brazil, Burma, or Mozambique, as they are for Italy, Spain, Rumania, or the UK. It should also be understood that such measures could only be implemented on a nation by nation basis not only because legal arrangements and institutions vary in every country, but because socio-economic conditions are different also.

In view of this, the vital role of the Nationality principle can be comprehended in challenging the power of globalisation. The core purpose of the Nationality principle is that every nation state must take ultimate responsibility for its own problems, which of course calls for democracy in fulfilling the best needs of the majority. The principle lays emphasis on the common sense notion of self-sustainability, and as a logical consequence of this, it deplores mass population movements from one territory to another for whatever reason.

If the reason is political then those who wish to free their native land should have the courage and nous to join or found law-abiding protest or petitioning movements. In an age when there are many international agencies for overseeing justice in all parts of the world, there is no longer an excuse for betraying the cause of one's people by flight and exile. If the reason is economic then the discontented should call on their government to promote productivity and trade. If the reasons are due to environmental erosion, water shortages, or over-population, or a combination of these factors, then the government should call for international aid and promote effective population control policies, whilst also being responsible to containing their people within national boundaries.

The movement of population masses has always upset the territorial arrangements of peoples, and in the past has brought even great civilisations to their fall. I first called attention to the ills of allowing unfettered freedom of movement between states more than 45 years ago in a lecture attended by a significant body of the diplomatic corps and other prominent citizens, delivered to the International Society in Helsinki, in January 1964. Those views I still retain, since they are more urgently relevant today than they were then, and the lecture was recently re-printed in my book, *Land of The Olympians*.

10 – An expanding circle of international cooperation

A further essential step is the international role of cooperation and friendship between friendly states. In this sphere, the first step is the identity of similar economies, and the meeting of leading personalities keen on establishing a Social capitalist world. The first countries to initiate such moves would naturally be those most industrially advanced, since their middle-middle majorities would sooner have developed a social consciousness for advancing such ideas. In order of forming into an expanding international movement, the following pattern might emerge:- in the first wave: the north west European countries together with the Far East Tigers of Japan, Korea, Singapore, Taiwan, and Australia and New Zealand, and the People's Republic of China as a friendly associate; in the second wave: the Mediterranean European countries and Malaysia, Thailand, the Philippines, Vietnam, and Cambodia; in the third wave: the countries of Eastern Europe and South America; in the fourth wave: Russia, Ukraine, and the central Asian states including Mongolia; in the fifth wave: central America, Indonesia, and the countries of the Middle East; in the sixth wave: India, north and sub-Saharan Africa; and finally, in the seventh wave: the USA, in liberating her people from the shackles of economic oppression.

The above order is not intended to reflect any bias of favour, and neither is it intended to reflect organisational purpose, but rather as a prediction of preparedness towards friendly cooperation. There may be many countries in the above list which do not seem to have been included in a particular category. If this has been so, it was not intended. There are other categories which have been left intentionally vague, e.g., the Middle East. It may be noted there are deep divisions between the Arab states, Israel, and Iran. These raise questions which currently are irresolvable, and must pass without comment, as far as the limitations of this book are concerned.[14]

The proposed associate membership of China is made in the light of her status as by far the most productive country on earth, and consequently, the weight of her economic power cannot be compared with that of any other nation state. Out of

---

[14] With regard to the Israeli-Palestinian conflict, readers may like to consult chapter 6 of my book, *Freedom From America*, for a consideration of this problem.

respect in acknowledging her exceptional position, it has to be assumed she would not deign to compromise her honour by joining a federation of "minor states" intent on measures of self-protection against the usury of another power.

Geo-politics is more significantly about power than any other branch of politics, and so why should China bow her head in a gesture whereby she might be expected to compromise her interests? Likewise, why should the other advanced industrial countries of the world embarrass their self-esteem by approaching her as a suppliant? There may be disagreement on both sides with regard to developing economic policies of one kind or another, but in any event the world needs China as an invaluable ally as well as a vital trading partner. As the oldest and one of the greatest civilisations on the planet, her Confucian culture and rational ways of life have much to commend to the other peoples of the world. In Europe, already by the mid-18th century, leading opinion-formers admired the wisdom, civility, and equable nature of her society as suitable for emulation, comparing it unfavourably with the vanity and often chaotic politics of the West. The purpose of associate membership is therefore intended to openly explore avenues for mutual exchange and cooperation in any desirable sphere of activity.

11 – Dissolving conglomerates but encouraging incoming investment

In taking realistic steps to strengthen the home-based or *real* (as contrasted with the *phony*) economy, in promoting longer term and full employment policies, as well as in strengthening the conditions for civic and democratic life, brief mention is made of sidestepping the City institutions. It is suggested that minimal *direct* intervention be made by government with regard to the international business of the City, although the *indirect* influence may be considerable over a period of time.

This would arise, firstly, through the establishment (or enhancement) of financial institutions, both at home and abroad, for the sole purpose of promoting domestic productivity, and hence the emergence of two parallel but nonetheless touching economies; secondly, through the legislation of nation states in financially inspecting and dissolving conglomerates into their earlier independent ownership enterprises; thirdly, through proclaiming the illegality of offshore tax havens,[15] or other agencies used for such a purpose, and in practice this would entail the seizure by governments of those companies and their assets within their territoriality for transfer to the ownership of locally based CEOs; and fourthly, the implications of legislation arising from changes to Company law in regard to employee share-ownership and management control.

Although the City institutions would not be in a position to object to, or hinder, any of the above proposals since firstly, such proposals are geared to financially benefit the majority, and secondly, they anyway only entail *indirect* intervention, they nonetheless raise many legal and economic issues which need to be anticipated and resolved before practical reforms are set in place. But if those with sufficient skill and good intentions are called upon to undertake the task, success will be the outcome.

As I have stated in earlier books, no barriers should be placed on foreign enterprises planting their roots in Britain, or in any other territory, providing the returns are profitable to the host country either in raising what is judged to be sufficient taxable income, or in the employment of local labour. On the other hand, there are occasions when objections may be raised by any nation state to the exploitation of low labour costs. Although it is often impracticable or futile to challenge such a situation, e.g., when confronting an economy of exceptional size, except through import duties and substitution as outlined above; there are other situations when a challenge may be met. For example, an undesirable situation could be deemed to arise when wealthy financial service institutions, or major utilities employ overseas tele-sales organisations, thereby promoting unemployment in the home country.

---

[15] Some commentators have even remarked (perhaps with tongue in cheek) that the City of London is the largest and most notorious tax haven of all.

12 – A Federation of Social Capitalist States

Having discussed the function of the Nationality principle in empowering effectively through democratic means the best interests of majorities, we must now turn to the role of an International Federation of Social Capitalist States. Such a federation may indeed be preceded by an association propagating the formulated principles, but only a federation of governments leading Social Capitalist States can hope to exert the formidable political authority desired. Such a federation would aim at forming a powerful politico-economic bloc between America, identified as a dire agency undermining justice, equity, and democracy worldwide; and China, identified as a nation wavering between two economic ideologies, and sought as a partner for dialogue and friendship.

The purpose of such a federation would be to promote trade amongst its members along the principles described above; enlarge its membership globally; promote the economic and cultural integrity of its members through disengaging from America in the spheres of military and political cooperation – except in an international emergency; and minimising financial, commercial, and cultural links with that country. Mutual cooperation and exchange with America should be actively promoted in the spheres of academia, science, information technology and space development, high culture, and the printing and distribution of books, and commercial propositions stemming *directly* from these activities (subject to their acceptance by responsible inspection bodies), but should be discouraged in other areas.

A function of the federation, transcending all others, would be the advancement of world peace and concord amongst peoples, achieved through the disinterested socio-economic principles of justice and equity assured through the mechanisms of what we have described as *Full* democracy. But as we have argued in earlier chapters, full democracy, or *total power* held by the community as *individuals*, is only open to those advanced industrialised societies which have evolved into new majorities mutating into the Responsible Society. And it is only the achievement of this which can come close to marking *The End of History* – if the arrogance of such a claim could ever be made.

13 – A new role for the great nations of the past

But the countries of north Western Europe, as well as the Confucian nations of the Far East, are already developing societies which closely approximate the ideal outcome of the Responsible Society. This is occurring through legislation, and that egalitarianism which springs as a natural consequence of technological development in the world of work. But the essential condition for achieving such a society, with the morality and happiness that follows in its wake, is a Productive economic system purged of the ills of usury.

This book may seemingly present a stance which is politically anti-American. Nothing is intended against the individual American, and the greatness of her achievements in the spheres of science and technology, and indeed the greatness of her literature and arts (unhappily concealed behind a mist of demeaning populism), is fully acknowledged. But the geo-political pattern of her imposing a usurious and socially oppressive financial-industrial system on the rest of the world, poses an intolerable situation which needs to be met by an anti-Americanism that is not gratuitous but springs from a moral imperative. In America this book is intended as a wake-up call in liberating her own people. It is therefore hoped it will be met in such a spirit. Anything less than candid anti-Americanism would be a cowardly retreat into futile discussions on socio-economic theory divorced from confronting concrete *actuality*.

The evidence is there – worldwide – for the harm that has been done, and is being done. In confronting practical reality, it is therefore necessary to strike directly at the source of the problem, and not out at a tangent to confuse or blur the clarity of the intended message. Naturally, political cooperation should be encouraged with like-minded American associations – of which there are plenty – for that would establish constructive dialogue.

In illustrating the crazy mismatch in the polarisation of earnings in the US, the following figures are startling: whilst in 2007 CEOs of major corporations were paid 344 times the pay of the average worker (whilst in 1980 they were only paid 42 times that of the average worker); in 2008 the total wealth of American families fell by $11 trn, an amount equal to the combined annual output of Germany, Japan and the UK. The following international comparisons are also instructive with regard to possible future tendencies: whilst CEOs at top US companies earn an average of $13.3 m per year (using 2004-2006 data), in Europe it is $6.6 m for chief executives, and in Japan it is $1.5 m.

Commenting on the above figures, Michael Sandel, Bass Professor of Government at Harvard University, posed the question, "Were executives less talented and hard-working than they are today? Or do pay differentials reflect contingencies unrelated to talents and skills?" He further remarked, "arguments about the rights and wrongs of economic arrangements often lead us back to fundamental questions of what people morally deserve and why."[16]

That most respected thinker, and grand old man of letters, Gore Vidal, recently denounced his countrymen in no uncertain terms, exclaiming, "one thing I have hated all my life are *liars* and I live in a nation of them. It was not always the case. I don't demand honour, that can be lies too. I don't say there was a golden age, but there was an age of general intelligence. ... Obama believes the Republican party is a party when in fact it's a mindset, like Hitler Youth, based on hatred – religious hatred, racial hatred. When you foreigners hear the word 'Conservative' you think of kindly old men hunting foxes. They're not, they're fascists. ... America has no intellectual class and is rotting away at a funereal pace. We'll have a military dictatorship fairly soon, on the basis that nobody else can hold everything together."[17] In view of the above, and the nature of America's financial-

---

[16] Michael Sandel, "Bankers on bail," *New Stateman*, 14th September 2009.

[17] Interview given at the Connaught Hotel, Mayfair, at the end of September 2009, "Gore Vidal: 'We'll Have a Dictatorship soon in the US,'" http://www.informationclearinghouse.info/article23595.htm

industrial institutions, as we have described them in earlier chapters, it is appalling that such a country has been allowed to dominate the world for so long a period.

On the other hand, if Michael Sandel, Gore Vidal, and others like them in America could influence public opinion and change the attitudes of their countrymen, then there would be some hope for a better future. If, better still, America was to transform her financial-industrial system from within, into a benign Productive capitalism, that would be the happiest outcome for us all. In such a situation, America might regain her benign reputation in the world – and deservedly so – but until that day, she remains a threat to all humankind beyond the frontiers of her giant continent.

There are countries in the world today which in the not too distant past either enjoyed a long imperial tradition, or else a long and glorious military reputation as their badge of honour. These countries may be Continental powers, or small island nations at opposite sides of the globe, and every country should be proud of its history and achievements. But the past belongs to yesterday, and the ideals of a former epoch may not be those of today. Nonetheless, these countries with a similar quality of energy and a special heritage should unite in sincerity and friendship for a common purpose.

That purpose is not the mean pursuit of self-interest or the chasing after financial gain, but the broader philanthropic purpose of creating a new imperium of social justice and equity for the peoples of the world oppressed through millennia of superstition, tyranny, and want. Such a purpose, added to that of meeting the challenge of climate change, is not only moral in its call to power, but educational and practical in pointing the way ahead. It calls for the intelligence and direction of those privileged to be born and nurtured amongst the most advanced peoples on our planet, and the call is imperative in the sense that if it is not met, or goes unheard, there are none who can fill the tasks so sorely needed.

In a recent and stirring article, Lord Howell, made some pithy observations before appealing for a new sense of national purpose, when he wrote, "the US remains a ... powerful nation, but its unipolar moment has passed. It no longer leads the world, because there is no single 'top dog' in the old sense. Pax Americana is no more; and Western hegemony is in severe decline. This is why it is surely time for a clean break, and a new strategic direction – or, at the very least, to answer some immediate and important questions for British foreign policy. ... Perhaps above all, do we have the right ministerial and administrative systems in London to adjust, flexibly and swiftly, to the new conditions, and the right balance and coordination between our major departments concerned with overseas affairs? ... A dispiriting picture emerges. At a time when we should be forging new alliances with the powers that will affect our destiny, when we should be vigorously promoting new and more flexible structures for the EU, when we should be building up the Commonwealth as the ideal soft power network of the future, at a time when we should be massively modernising our security forces to meet asymmetric threats, when we should be reconstructing and upgrading our whole diplomatic system, we are doing none of those things."[18]

Meanwhile, Martin Jacques, from the opposite end of the political divide, expresses similar sentiments on the *Dämmerung* or twilight of American power when he writes, "The financial crisis began in the United States. It has served to expose the deep flaws and falsities of US economic growth since the early 1990s. And it marks the collapse of the neoliberal ideology that has dominated Western thinking since the 1970s. In other words, it constitutes the most profound financial, economic, political and ideological crisis of the West since the 1930s. ... Not only are we in the midst of the biggest world economic recession since the 1930s, but we are also entering an entirely new global era. It marks the end of the Bretton Woods order and the US-made international economic and financial order. The US is no longer economically strong enough to sustain it. The basic cause of the financial crisis has been the weakening of the US, its

---

[18] David Howell, "British Diplomacy is in a disastrous state," *The Daily Telegraph*, 25th September 2009.

growing dependence on China, and the asset bubbles that this enabled. But if the American order is in its death throes, what might replace it?"[19]

The answer to this question is only to be found in the promise of a new imperium of enlightened countries, in both East and West, joining hands to form a power bloc of well-governed states for peace, social justice and equity for peoples across the globe. This would be the logical outcome of history, and mark the deserving role of those re-emerging powers which have already established their reputation as stable democracies.

Britain would only be one amongst a score of such countries with a special purpose to fulfil. All such countries with a glorious heritage are lost for a role to play in the years ahead. Their traditions and greatness in the past, shames them in the present, in the light of lost power and a lowly destiny. Their potential as being in the forefront, in holding in their grasp all spheres of knowledge and expertise, is their only promise for an honourable and fruitful posterity. In this alone, in following such a path, may they justify their past reputation through the present in the eyes of the watching and hopeful millions throughout the four corners of our planet.

***

---

[19] Martin Jacques, "No one rules the world," *New Statesman*, 30th March 2009.

A Guide to Further Reading

The following books not only set out to present a practical programme for the future, but more significantly, to create a new thinking or approach to political life for a just and upwardly aspiring egalitarian society. Perhaps more important still, they repudiate what has now become the self-destructiveness of the left/right divide. All the books cited below (which are written by Robert Corfe) are addressed to the enquiring general reader, no less than to the academic or specialist –

Emergence of The New Majority, being Volume I of *Social Capitalism in Theory and Practice*
ISBN 978-0-9556055-3-6   pp. xxxv/282   Royal Octavo
Notes, Appendices, Bibliography, Index

After analysing what should be the remit of political discussion in the *real* world, in differentiating between utopian and practical politics, the author describes the mismatch between the outdated mindset of political parties and the transformation of society and the world of work over the past 60 years. This has increasingly led to the compounding rather than the resolution of major political problems. The breakdown of the old middle and working classes and their values is traced historically, and it is shown that this was brought about through changing patterns of employment, legislation towards a more egalitarian society, and other economic factors.

The emergence of the new middle-middle majority, with its different values, occurred whilst the political establishment was hardly aware of the fact. Although this new class is highly heterogeneous, at the same time, its specific but unheeded economic needs will eventually act as a catalyst for change. As a new class consciousness emerges through the realisation of these needs, the middle-middle majority will mutate into the all-powerful Responsible Society. The book concludes by addressing several current issues as an exercise in applying Social Capitalist principles.

The People's Capitalism, being Volume II of *Social Capitalism in Theory and Practice*
ISBN 978-0-9556055-4-3   pp. xx/461   Royal Octavo
Notes, Appendices, Bibliography, Index

This book begins by examining the nature of power in the contemporary world: in the world of politics, and more significantly, in the financial-industrial sectors which dominates the first. It examines how power is exerted in the Third world, and compares this with power in the advanced industrial economies. The limits of democracy and federations in upholding the interests of majorities is pointed out, and there is a call for radical changes to the economic system. Part II is concerned with socialising Productive capitalism and how this may be achieved politically. Part III entails an in-depth analysis of Rentier and Productive capitalism: how they operate internationally, and comparisons of their benefits and disbenefits to society, and their differing macro-economic influences.

Part IV presents a pro-active strategy for the industrial trades unions in working to transform their employing enterprises from the Rentier to the Productive model. Part V on the Human Priorities of Politics delves into a number of philosophical and moral topics on society and government: e.g., on expediency versus justice; the self-justifying cynicism of vested interests; political realism in the just society; how to maximise the individual's potential; and, the desirable foundations for a disinterested politics. The book concludes with a description of the Responsible Society.

Prosperity in a Stable World, being Volume III of *Social Capitalism in Theory and Practice*
ISBN 978-0-9556055-5-0   pp. xx/473   Royal Octavo
Notes, Appendices, Bibliography, Indices

The book opens with 7 chapters on redefining the benefits of free trade in a world dominated by Productive capitalist economies. In such a world legislation would be in place to ensure that international trade was equitable and non-exploitative. There would be an end to usurious lending or investments, and instead, structures would be put in place for releasing the dead capital of the poor through extra-legal arrangements. The new practices of free trade would be linked into meeting the needs of the environment.

Part II is concerned with strategies for national prosperity, and describes the essential basics for a just economy in very simple terms. Such concepts as productivity, wealth creation, and ownership as a stewardship, are given precise definitions. Government policies for industry, and new modes for funding enterprises are covered in detail. Part III is concerned with job creation for Social Wealth. It begins by differentiating between Social and Unsocial Wealth Creation, and describes how industry and jobs have been undermined by Rentier capitalistic practices. Towards correcting the imbalance between public and private sectors, occupational priorities are listed according to productivity; the invisible barriers to trade are identified; and proposals are put forward for reversing manufacturing decline, together with special legislation in increasing the profitability of the productive sector.

Part IV on reforming the business enterprise is concerned with the nature of the Company: identifying its intrinsic purpose; fairness and efficiency as one; and a proposed General Purposes clause for the company. There is also a chapter which discusses the different concepts of usury and as to their relevance today. Part V: Forty-Three Failing Britain, an exercise in the critique of Rentier capitalism, is an attack on a powerful group of corporate directors following their letter published in

The Times shortly before a general election. Part VI concludes the book with a 49-page Declaration of Social Capitalist Values.

Egalitarianism of The Free Society *and the end of class conflict*
ISBN 978-0-9556055-2-9   pp. xviii/317   Royal Octavo
Notes, Bibliography, Index

This book is an adjunct to *Social Capitalism in Theory and Practice*, in that it expands on several subordinate yet important themes raised in the 3-volume work. Part I comprises 6 chapters on the relationship between Culture and Egalitarianism. Then follow 11 chapters on the Politics of Property which examine the psychological nature of possession, and in pursuing the argument of one of the greatest 19th century philosophers, the author demonstrates that the individual can only reach his full potential through the ownership and use of property.

Property is then described in the different forms in which it occurs in society, including communal and collective property. Part III, Democracy: Real and Illusory, begins by outlining the erosion of freedom in the contemporary world, followed by a clear differentiation between the democratic way of life and democratic government, and how the one may exist without the other. For example, whilst India purports to have a democratic government, its society is the least democratic imaginable. Singapore, on the other hand, has an ideally democratic and multi-racial society, but its government tends towards authoritarianism. Several commonly held beliefs about British democracy are exploded, and there is a discussion as to when the benefits of democracy are maximised.

The book concludes with 12 chapters on the Road to Constructive Politics, being a critique of 20th century epistemological theories and practices, acting as a barrier to constructive thought. In the revolt against reason, philosophical pragmatism is targeted for particular criticism. The nature of reason is examined, and the reality of ideas is upheld as an essential tool for the intelligent discussion of the material world.

The book concludes with an appeal for establishing a New Idealism, the proponents of which would use a methodology very different from their predecessors.

The Death of Socialism *the irrelevance of the traditional left and the call for a progressive politics of universal humanity*
ISBN 978-1-906791-14-2   pp. xvi/174   Demy 8vo
Notes, Index

The author wrote this book after 14 years as an activist, both locally and nationally as a Labour party member. He describes his efforts to update the thinking and attitudes of the party to fit the needs of today's contemporary majority. With this in mind, he attempted to establish a New Socialism, which would not only be more objective in outlook but eschew class-based prejudices. The purpose of politics in the 21st century, surely, was not to nurture old resentments or fight old battles, but to resolve substantive issues in creating a just and egalitarian society.

Although Labour party members today rarely openly promote the idea of class struggle, the author discerned a deeply-felt psychological attitude which was more concerned with "knocking" the opposition than resolving difficult issues for the benefit of all society. Worse still, the attitudes and actions of the Labour party and socialism betray they are not fighting for a classless all-inclusive society, but rather for a proletarian society modelled after their own ideals in discriminating against the rest of the population. The final chapters of the book argue it is necessary to transcend the self-destructive conflicts of the past, through practical politics ensuring an all-inclusive society for justice and equity for all.

Populism Against Progress and the collapse of aspirational values
ISBN 978-0-9543161-8-1   pp. xviii/152   Demy 8vo
Notes, Index

This book opens with a description of the hidden poison of populism which is not only undermining democracy but threatens to destroy Western civilisation. In the second chapter this is contrasted with the beneficent power of culture with its channels for creativity on one hand, and bonding mechanisms for understanding and communication on the other. There then follow chapters on the populism of Islamic fundamentalism and how this is hindering the progress of their own people; the battle for freedom through education; social bonding through cultural education; and how populism is adversely affecting the achievement of an upwardly aspiring egalitarian society.

This leads to considering the self-destructiveness of contemporary politics, followed by chapters on corporate power and the corruption of society, and the debasement of culture through marketing strategies. The book concludes with a consideration of those philosophical and educational influences which may be called upon to combat populism and promote higher aspirational values.

Deism and Social Ethics the role of religion in the third millennium
ISBN 978-0-9543161-9-8   pp. xx/201   Demy 8vo
Notes, Appendix, Bibliography, Index

Following a period earlier in the 20th century when it was assumed that secularism had finally come to dominate political life worldwide, in the 21st century we now find ourselves living in a very different environment. The influence of religion in political life is now becoming increasingly significant in many parts of the world. In those areas where majorities are more intellectually developed, i.e., in Western Europe and the

Confucian countries of the Far East, secularism remains firm in politically guiding the future.

Two questions are raised in this book: firstly, it has now been physiologically demonstrated that the religious temperament is an essential part of the human psyche (although differing in intensity from one person to another) and hence it is ineradicable. The issue in the modern world, therefore, arises as to the desirability of religion without superstition or revelation. The second question arises as how best to communicate with those regimes dominated by religion when the latter is the only basis for personal trust. The author argues for integrity and truth in considering religious questions, as otherwise insincerity and falsehood may lead to mistrust and the failure of political negotiations in the international sphere.

The book presents the need for the deistic beliefs of the early 18th century, but updated with regard to defining the nature of the deity. It promotes a form of deism, based on reason and philosophical principles, enabling a first step on the ladder of religion without commitment to myth, superstition or theology.

Deism as an approach to religion would therefore ideally fulfil the healthy sceptical needs and love of freedom, of enlightened humankind in the third millennium. Meanwhile, in the realm of diplomacy, in acknowledging with conviction the existence of God, it would help bring different faiths towards a common political purpose. The book also presents a critical review and appreciation of leading faiths throughout the world.

Freedom From America *for safeguarding democracy and the economic and cultural integrity of peoples*
ISBN 978-0-9543161-5-0   pp. xviii/222   Demy 8vo
Notes, Appendices, Index
(Also available in Arabic, published by Da-Al-Salam in Cairo)

The book opens with the contention that "the American mindset is distinct from that of any other people or race on earth in a way that no other peoples or races are distinct from one another." Whilst acknowledging that America has produced valued bodies of specialised learning and research, and assenting with G.K. Chesterton's quip, that "the real American is all right; it is only the ideal American who is all wrong," the author then begins to analyse these false values which have made the American character. These stem from a particular type of materialism, whereby money and its acquisition is put on a pedestal above human and other values. This has led inevitably not only to an extreme form of greed, but to deceit and the disguising of motives and attitudes in the service of material gain. These unpleasant characteristics are in turn covered up by a false amiability and superficiality in human relationships.

Out of such a society has developed a highly sophisticated Rentier capitalistic system offering a wide range of usurious financial products. The opening chapter describes an international situation whereby America finds herself versus the rest of the world, in terms of corporate power, and a political ideology convinced it has a God-given mission to culturally absorb all peoples throughout the planet. Chapter 2 is concerned with America and the Deception of the World; Chapter 3 is entitled America and the Debasement of Cultural Values; and Chapter 4, America and the Debasement of Democratic Values, through the emergence of the plutocratic state.

The last two chapters discuss ways in which the world may be liberated from American hegemony. Chapter 5 is entitled, A Global Strategy for the Planet and Humankind, in considering environmental issues in addition to an enlightened business culture, and the need to confront America as an ethical imperative. The last chapter, De-Fusing the Causes of Terror, investigates the injustice and anarchy in many parts of the world stemming directly from American intervention, either direct or covert through such agencies as the CIA. World terrorism can never be defeated through the American war machine – although it may be worsened. It can only be defeated through enabling justice and granting national rights to oppressed peoples.

Our Swindling Finance Houses their exploitation of the *vulnerable*
ISBN 978-0-9538460-5-4   pp. xxi/121   Demy 8vo

Using the pseudonym of Guy Tallice, the author describes his horrific 6-month stint in working for a major finance services company, and household name, at the end of the 1980s. Having been made redundant as a senior executive of a manufacturing enterprise, and desperate to find work to keep up mortgage payments, and maintain a family with 3 young children, he joined Allied Dunbar as a Sales Associate.

The book opens with a Preface sub-headed Swindling Within The Law, which examines in some detail different modes of fraud and sleight of hand used to confuse or deceive the public. He shows how financial services use swindling methods throughout the industry, and concludes with an appeal for legislation to define and make swindling an illegal activity. He then vividly describes the guile of recruitment methods, and the ingenuity of deceit in inveigling the unemployed into their organisation.

During the Thatcherite era when industries were going bust and unemployment was soaring, there were only Phony Jobs in A Phony World, being the title of the opening chapter. The second chapter, Ripe for Exploitation, describes in detail the pain of unemployment together with its adverse psychological effect on the personality, and the stress it brings to family life. The third chapter, What Dreams are Made of, describes the recruiting procedures, with promises of riches for those working for the company. The fourth chapter, The Glory Days, outlines the author's working experience and early success.

Using hard-selling methods, after an intensive training course, he approached every relative, friend, neighbour, and casual acquaintance, to buy Personal Pension plans. In addition, he approached industrial enterprises, and in one factory sold personal pension plans to a number of semi-literate manual workers on the minimum legal wage. Back at the office he was held up by the branch manager as an example of the ideal Sales Associate. The author, however, could meanwhile not understand the downcast attitude and apparent apathy of colleagues – or not until it was too late.

The subsequent chapters expose the huge swindle inflicted on Sales Associates, each of whom supposedly had a separate and secret arrangement with his manager on the mode of remuneration. The author called a meeting of his colleagues and they cooperated in a rescue plan for disengagement from the company, meeting secretly in the office late in the evening, and using available facilities in photocopying CVs in an attempt to find real jobs. Although the author was never paid the commission he had earned, and incurred heavy debts by the time he left the company, he escaped lightly by comparison with several colleagues who lost their homes and personal assets, due to extortionate loans forced on them by managers to maintain business and living costs.

When the swindle was finally uncovered, the author turned on his colleagues, asking why they had not warned him of the fraud into which they had all fallen. Their simple answer was: "But we all had our different arrangements and we didn't know what yours were. When the mask was taken off we just felt stupid. Now don't you feel the same?" – "No," replied the author, "I just feel swindled." Drawing together all the facts, he wrote to Sir Mark Weinberg, Chairman of the company who had been knighted the previous years at the instigation of Margaret Thatcher for developing the financial services industry. The letter was copied to several other directors. The letters went unacknowledged, but the matter was passed to senior managers who called a meeting to talk through the problem, but despite flattering gestures, discussions ended in futile circular arguments.

The author's career with Allied Dunbar was brought to a sudden halt following serious injuries during a crash as a front seat car passenger, after signing up a major contract with an engineering company, together with a senior colleague, as they sped away at high speed in elated spirits, realising they would shortly be £4,000 richer. After 3 years litigation, the author was persuaded (through the burden of debts) to accept a derisory compensation payment from the company for his injuries. Shortly after hospitalisation, the author visited his remaining colleagues in their office to be cheerfully met with the revelation that Allied Dunbar had arranged for them to receive Social Security benefits. And these were the employees of one of the wealthiest financial services institutions in the UK!

The final chapter proposes reforms in cleaning up the industry. In the first print run of the book there was, absurdly, a Dedicatory Petition to the Labour Government elected into power on 7th June 2001, to "initiate legislation to curb the greed dishonesty and scams of the financial institutions." It was not fully realised at the time that the Labour government would promote the interests to the usurious economy to Thatcherite proportions.

Land of The Olympians *papers from the enlightened Far North*
ISBN 978-1-906791-17-7   pp. 264   Royal Octavo
Notes, Index

This book reprints articles originally published in the 1960s in the Finnish press and learned journals, during the author's 10-year residence in Scandinavia. The leading series of 8 articles, *How To Be An Olympian*, were published in the country's leading intellectual journal, and comprise a study of neutrality in Sweden and Finland and how it affected social and political attitudes. The author praises the cool objectivity and sagacity of neutral Scandinavians in their socio-political outlook, comparing this favourably with the stressful, excitable, and often prejudicial environment of those countries unhappily caught up in the Russo-American conflict.

Here was a haven of peace, security, and sanity, in a world which was otherwise constantly in fear of nuclear war. The author raises the question of Britain and Continental Europe forming into a neutral but militarily powerful bloc, possibly at the instigation of Gaullist France, as a defence against the ideological fanaticism of Russo-America. Two other series of articles, published in Finland's second largest daily, comprise studies of the entrenched English class system, comparing it with the egalitarian and democratic societies of Scandinavia, with their higher living standards and greater freedom.

Other articles (several of which were illustrated with cartoons) take a wryly humorous look at Finnish life; and then there is a short story, *What The Watchdog Saw*, being a savage satire on the skulduggery of both the left and right in the Britain of the 1960s. The book concludes with a lecture, *Internationalism and Europe*, originally delivered in 1964, in which the author argues that Europe is ideally placed, through her greater maturity, to take realistic measures for establishing a more peaceful world in intervening between the abrasive political extremism of two larger powers.

The Social Capitalist Network
www.socialcapitalistnetwork.org

**

Robert Corje@ tiscali, co.uk

INDEX